NUMBER 696

THE ENGLISH EXPERIENCE

ITS RECORD IN EARLY PRINTED BOOKS
PUBLISHED IN FACSIMILE

ROBERT SOME

A GODLY TREATISE...
TOUCHING THE
MINISTERIE, SACRAMENTS,
AND CHURCH

LONDON, 1588

WALTER J. JOHNSON, INC.
THEATRUM ORBIS TERRARUM, LTD.
AMSTERDAM 1974 NORWOOD, N.J.

The publishers acknowledge their gratitude to
the Syndics of Cambridge University Library
for their permission to reproduce parts of the
Library's copy, Shelfmark Dd.4.15^6(E) and to
the Dean and Chapter of Peterborough Cathedral
for their permission to reproduce parts of the
Library's copy, Shelfmark Pet.G.6.12^1.

S.T.C. No. 22909

Collation: A-E^4, F^2, G-Z^4, Aa-Bb^4, Cc^2

Published in 1974 by

Theatrum Orbis Terrarum, Ltd.
O.Z. Voorburgwal 85, Amsterdam

&

Walter J. Johnson, Inc.
355 Chestnut Street
Norwood, New Jersey
07648

Printed in the Netherlands

ISBN 90 221 0696 9

Library of Congress Catalog Card Number:
74-80231

GODLY TREATISE

containing and deciding certaine
queſtions, mooued of late in London and
other places, touching the Miniſterie,
Sacraments, and Church.

Whereunto one Propoſition more is added.

After the ende of this Booke you ſhall
finde a defence of ſuch points as M. Penry
hath dealt againſt: And a confutation of many groſſe errours broched
in M. Penries laſt
Treatiſe.

Written by Robert Some Doctor
of Diuinitie.

Epheſ. 4. verſe 15.
Let vs follow the trueth in loue, and in all things grow
vp into him, which is the head (that is) Chriſt, &c.

Imprinted at London by G. B. Deputie to Chri-
ſtopher Barker, Printer to the Queenes moſt excellent Maieſtie. 1588.

¶ To the Reader.

Wo fortes of Recufantes are in this land:
the one Popifh, the other Anabaptifticall.
They giue out,that wee haue no miniftery,
no Sacraments, no vifible Church. Thefe
men labour of two difeafes:the one is great
pride, the other groffe ignorance. Their
pride appeares in their behauiour,which is voide of humilitie:
their ignorance in their Arguments, which hang together
like a ficke mans dreame.That her Maieftie may and ought to
compell thefe Recufants to frequent our Church affemblies,
I make no queftion. There is an other forte,which either deny or doubt,whether vnpreaching minifters doe deliuer a Sacrament : vpon better aduife, fome of them confeffe, that ignorant minifters,doe adminifter a Sacrament: but they adde
this, that fuch as receiue any Sacrament at their hands, doe
finne groffely and pollute thefelues.I will hope well of thefe
men : for they erre, onely for want of iudgement. The holy
Sacrament is one thing, the minifters ignorance is an other
thing : the Lordes Sacrament brings finguler comfort to the
worthie receiuer : the minifters ignorance can neither peruert the Sacrament,nor pollute the receiuer. The Donatiftes
taught otherwife in the former time, and the Anabaptiftes
in our time : but they are notably confuted by two famous
men,Auguftine and Caluine. What account I make of ignorant minifters,appeareth in this treatife.It pleafed God
to direct my heart and penne in this holy labour:
therefore I affure my felfe of his gracious
bleffing. *London,May. 6.*
1 5 8 8.

R. S.

A Table of such points as are contei-
ned in this Treatise.

1. A GODLY PRINCE

may and ought to compell his Subiects (if any refuse) to the externall Seruice of God.

IT is the Princes duetie to prouide able men to teache the Lordes Religion in his dominions. So did Iosaphat the king of Iuda. *2.Chro.17.* and Artaxerxes the king of Persia. *Ezra 7.* therefore, it is the Princes duetie, to prouide that his Subiects doe heare and learne the Lords religion. Teachers and learners are relatiues.

Great outrages were committed against both the tables of the commandements, as appeareth in the booke of Iudges: *for, euery man did that which was good in his owne eyes: Iudg.17. & 19.cha.* The reason of these absurdities is set out liuely and often in these words: *There was no king in Israel. Iudg.17.18. & 19.Chap.* by which words it is manifest, that if a religious Prince had bene in place, Idolatrie and wicked behauiour had bene suppressed, and the Israelites pressed to serue the Lorde. That Princes doe not passe their bounds in this, it is cleare by that which Augustine reporteth of and commendeth in the King of Babylon. *Contra Cresc.gram.lib.3.cap.51.*

The Prince is bound to sanctifie the Sabboth: so are his subiects: the Lords commaundement is flat for this: *Remember the Sabboth day, to keepe it holy: Sixe*

dayes

dayes *shalt thou labour,and do all thy worke: But the seuenth day is the Sabbath of the Lord thy God,in it thou shalt not do any worke, thou, nor thy sonne,nor thy daughter, thy man seruant,nor thy mayd,nor thy beast,nor thy stranger that is within thy gates,&c.Exo. 20.*If none are exempted by almightie God,none can be dispensed with by man, for all are charged to present themselues in the holy assemblies. And, least any, either prince or subiect, should forget this duetie, the Lord himselfe is their remembrancer in these wordes : *Remember,that thou sanctifie the Sabboth &c.* that is, the sanctification of my Sabboth, is a matter very important, it concerneth my honour,but thy comfort,therfore remember and forget it not. If any refuse, they may and ought to bee compelled :for the breach of the Sabboth is a hainous sinne.*Iere.17.Nehem.13.*

Faith commeth by hearing of the word, *Rom.10.* therefore refusall to heare, hinders both the beginning and growth of faith. The Samaritanes heard Philippe in Samaria: they beleeued, *Actes 8.* Lydia heard Paul at Philippos : she beleeued, *Act.16.* Augustine was a Manichee nine yeeres : he heard Ambrose the Bishop of Mediolanum, and was conuerted. *Augusti.confess.lib.4.cap.1.and lib.5.cap.13.and 14.* If any shal aske me why all that heare,beleeue not:I answere,*Arcana Dei sunt adoranda,non scrutanda:* That is, Gods secrets are not to be searched, but adored: and,that vnlesse Gods spirit touch the heart, as the worde doeth pearce the eare, Gods holy Trueth is a dead letter vnto vs.

Asa,Iosias,were famous kings of Iuda. Asa commāded Iuda to seeke the Lord God of their fathers, and to do according to the law and cōmandement,

2.Chron.

2.Chron.14. Iosias compelled his subiects to serue the Lord their God,*2.Chron.34.* So did Manasses after his conuersion. *2.Chron.33.* If it were lawfull for these Kings of Iuda, to cōmaund and compell their subiects, it is not vnlawfull for ours to do the like. If it be not lawfull to compell recusants, why are Asa, Iosias, Manasses, commended by the holy Ghost for this excellent course?

Ezra was a learned Scribe : he was authorized by the King of Persia, to teache them beyonde the riuer Euphrates the Lavve of God, vvhich did not knowe it, and to punish such as refused to learne. Artaxerxes vvarrant is set dovvne in this sort ; *And thou Ezra (after the wisdome of thy God, that is in thine hand,) set Iudges and arbiters, which may iudge all the people that is beyonde the riuer, euen all that knowe the Lawe of thy God, and teache yee them that knowe it not : And whosoeuer will not doe the Lawe of thy God, and the Kings lawe, let him haue iudgement without delay, whether it be vnto death, or to banishment, or to confiscation of goods, or to imprisonment. Esra.7.verse 25,26.* And least any should take exception against Artaxerxes commaundement, Ezra cleareth it of all suspition of vnlavvfulnesse, in these vvordes : *Blessed bee the Lorde God of our fathers, which hath inclined the Kings heart to beautifie the House of the Lorde that is in Ierusalem. Ezra 7. verse 27.*

Augustine the Bishoppe of Hippo in Africke, vvas a very famous man: hee vvas sometimes of opinion, that heretiques vvere to bee pressed by argument, and not by the Magistrate: his reason then vvas, *Ne fictos Catholicos haberemus, quos apertos hereticos noueramus,* That is, least vvee should haue them

in

counterfait Catholiques , whome wee knewe to
bee notorious heretiques. But after weightie confideration, hee chaunged his former opinion, and
is very refolute, that Recufants may and ought to
bee compelled by the Magiftrate. *Auguft.Epift.48.
204.*

*Si terrerentur & non docerentur, improba quafi domi-
natio videretur: Sed rurfus, Si docerentur, & non terrerentur,&c. Auguft.Epift.48.* that is, to punifh and not
to teach, were tyrannie : againe, to teach and not to
punifh, were to harden them in their auncient cu-
ftome, and to make them flowe to enter the path of
faluation.

*Exi in vias & fepes, & compelle intrare, Luke 14. Qui
compellitur, quò non vult cogitur: fed quùm intrauerit, iam
volens pafcitur. Auguft.Epift.204.* that is, Go out into
the high wayes, and hedges, and compell them to
come in: he that is compelled, is compelled to enter
againft his will : but when hee is entred, hee is fedde
willingly.

*Ad cænam tanti patrisfamilias, fi fponte non vultis,
intrare compellimus. Auguft.contra. 2. Gaudentij Epift.
lib.2.cap.28.* that is, to the fupper of fo great an houfe-
holder, if you wil not of your owne accord, we compell you to enter.

*Quod autem vobis videtur, inuitos ad veritatem non
effe cogendos, &c. Auguft. contra 2. Gaudentij Epift.
lib.2.cap.17.* That is, where as yee thinke, that men
are not to bee compelled to the Trueth againft
their vvilles, yee erre, not knovving the Scriptures,
nor the povver of G o d, vvhich maketh thofe vvil-
ling , though they bee compelled againft their
willes.

Qui

Qui phreneticum ligat, & lethargicum excitat, ambo-
bus molestus, ambos amat. Aug.Epist.48. That is, he that
bindeth a frantike man, and awaketh him that
hath the lethargy, loueth both,
though he be grieuous
to both.

2. A GODLY PRINCE MAY

not suffer any religion but the true religion, either
publikely or priuately in his Dominions.

He exercife of falfe religion is directly
againft the fanctification of the Lords
Sabboth: *Exo.20.* therefore the Prince
may not at any hande fuffer it. The
Morall lawe, as it teacheth the wor-
fhip of Almightie God in the firft, and honeftie of
life in the fecond table of the commandements, is
perpetuall, and bindeth vs vnto the worldes ende.

The Ifraelites being in captiuitie in Egypt, were
required by Pharao to facrifice to Almightie God
in Egypt: Mofes refufed &c. *Exod.8.* The Ifraelites
being in captiuitie in Babylon were required by the
Chaldeans to fing one of the fongs of Sion. They
refufed and anfwered thus: *How fhall we fing the Lords*
fong in a ftrange land? Pfal.137. Of thefe places I gather
my argument thus: It was not lawfull to facrifice in
Egypt, and to fing the Lords fong in *Chaldea*, which
were polluted landes: therefore it is not lawfull to
fuffer Idolatrous & popifh feruice in Englãd, which
is a holy land. That profeffed papifts are Idolaters,
it is manifeft: firft, they worfhip falfe gods: for they
worfhip Angels and Saintes deceafed which are no

B.i.   gods.

gods, Secondly, they worſhippe not the true God aright: for they doe not worſhip him according to his written worde.

Confeſſion & conſent in the true religion, is *Vinculum eccleſiæ*, the chaine and bond of Gods Church: for the Apoſtle faith, *there is but one faith.Ephe,4.5.* therefore diſſenſion and difference in religion is a diſſolutiō of Gods Church. But no prince may haue any, either hand or litle finger in diſſoluing Gods Church: for Kings and Queenes are the nurſing fathers and mothers of the Church.*Eſai.4.9.*

It is the Princes duetie to prouide for the ſafetie of the bodies, therefore much more for the ſafety of the ſoules of his ſubiects. If for the ſafetie of their ſoules, then they may not ſuffer them to poyſon their ſoules. True religion is the foode of the ſoule. It is but one. To ſwarue from that, is the bane of the ſoule. It leadeth to hell. The Shipmaſter and ſhepheard muſt keepe his ſhippe and ſheepe from rocke and wolfe, *Qui non ſeruat ſi poteſt periturum, occidit.*

The prince is bounde to ſerue the Lord in feare. *Pſal.2.* therefore he may not ſuffer almightie God to be diſhonoured by any of his ſubiects. God is notably diſhonoured, when falſe worſhip is ſuffered either publikely or priuately.

The Angel of the Church of Pergamus is reproued by Chriſt for hauing ſuch in Pergamus as maintained the doctrine of Balaam, and the doctrine of the Nicolaitans which God hated. The Angel of the Church of Thyatira is reproued by Chriſt for ſuffering Iezabel &c. to teach and to deceiue.*Apocal. 2.* therfore Princes ſinne grieuouſly which ſuffer the exerciſe of a falſe religion.

A godly

A godly prince may not ſuffer a wilfull breach of his owne lawes: therefore not of Gods lawes. Almightie God is greater then all Princes. His lawes doe as farre paſſe the princes, as the gold of Ophir the clay in the ſtreet.Beſides,they which hate Gods religion , and conſequently ſinne againſt the firſt table , are eaſily induced to diſobey their prince, which is a ſinne againſt the ſecond table. It was a famous ſpeech of the Emperour *Conſtantius* the father of *Conſtantinus* the Emperour : *Howe can they bee faſt and true to the Emperour , which are Traitours to Almightie God?Euſeb.lib.1.de vita Conſtant. King Aſa depoſed Maachah his mother from her regencie , becauſe ſhe had made an idoll in a groue: Aſa brake downe her idoll, and ſtamped it ,at the brooke Kidron.2.Chron.15.Ezechias* and *Ioſias* were famous Kings of Iuda.They deſtroyed the groues and temples of the idols . They tooke a direct courſe for Gods religion. Almightie God may not bee dalied with in his ſeruice. There muſt be no parting of ſtakes. Hee will either haue all or none. *Ezech.20.* The Lordes Altar and Baals Altar muſt not ſtand together. *Iudg.6.*

Nabuchodonoſor the king of Babylon made a decree,that euery people,nation and language,which ſpake any blaſphemie againſt the God of Sidrach, Miſach and Abednago,ſhould be drawen in pieces, and their houſes made a Iakes,&c.*Dan.3.*

Conſtantinus the Emperour did not ſuffer Idolatrie in any part of his dominions. *Euſeb.lib.4.de vita Conſt.* The Emperours *Theodoſius* and *Gratianus* did not ſuffer Arianiſme &c. *Theod. lib.5.cap.16.Sozom. lib.7.cap.12.and 4.*

Edward the ſixth, a Prince of famous memorie,

was dealt with by his honourable counsailours that the Lady Mary which succeeded in the kingdome, might haue popish masse &c. Arguments were vsed to induce his Maiestie to like of that course. His answere and resolution was negatiue. So doth master Foxe report in the Actes and monuments in these wordes: In the dayes of King Edward the sixth, *Carolus* the Emperour made requeft to the sayde King and his Counsell, to permit Lady Mary (who after succeeded in the crowne) to haue Masse in her house without preiudice of the Law. And the Counsel on a time sitting vpon matters of policie, hauing that in question, sent Cranmer then Archbishop of Canterburie, and Ridley then Bishop of London, to intreate the king for the same : who comming to his Grace, alledged their reasons and perswasions for the accomplishing thereof. So the King hearing what they could say, replied his answere againe out of the scriptures, so groundedly, grauely and fully, that they were enforced to giue place to his replication, and grant the same to be true. Then they, after long debating in this maner with his Maiestie, laboured politikely in an other fort, and alledged what dangers the denying thereof might bring to his grace, what breach of amitie of the Emperours part, what troubles, what vnkindnesse, and what occasions fundry wayes it woulde enforce &c. Vnto whome the king answered, willing them to content themselues: for he would (he saide) spende his life and all he had, rather then to agree and graunt to that hee knewe certainely to bee against the trueth. The which when the Bishops heard, notwithstanding they vrged him still to graunt, and would by

no

no meanes haue his nay. Then the good king feeing
their importunate fuite, that needes they woulde
haue his Maieftie to confent thereto, in the ende his
tender heart burfting out in bitter weeping and
fobbing, defired them to be content. Whereat the
Bifhoppes themfelues, feeing the kings zeale and
conftancie, wept as faft as he, and fo tooke their
leaue of his grace: and comming from him, the
Archbifhoppe tooke mafter Cheeke his Schoole-
mafter by the hand and fayde: Ah mafter Cheeke,
you may be glad all the dayes of your life, that you
haue fuch a fcholler, for he hath more diuinitie in
his litle finger then all we haue in all our bodies &c.
Thus farre mafter Foxe.

3. ABLE TEACHERS OVGHT
to be prouided (fo much as can be) for the Chur=
ches.

Ods people are the Lordes fheepe,
fpoufe, citie: therefore they muft be
fedde, garnifhed, watched ouer, with
the Lords foode, furniture, weapons.
This cannot bee done without able
teachers.

The worke of the minifterie is a famous worke.
Ephe.4. It paffeth Mofes Tabernacle, and Salomons
Temple: therefore it is to be committed to fkilfull
and faithfull men : by it Dagon, Diana are caft
downe, and the Lords Arke and religion are fet vp:
by it ignorance, darkenes, are remoued, and knowledge and light are planted: by it, many wandring
fheepe are brought to the Lords folde, and many

fheaues

sheaues of corne into the Lords barne. This appea-
peared notably in Samaria, Ephefus, Corinth, &c.

The Ambaffadors of earthly Princes, either are
or fhould be men of choife: otherwife, they difhonour their Princes, and become ridiculous: therefore, the minifters which are the Ambaffadors of
the higheft prince, *Mal.2.2.Cor.5.* muft haue fome
mettall in them. If they haue not, howe either can,
or fhall they deliuer the Lords commiffion?

A learned teacher is a fingular bleffing: for hee
feedeth Gods people with knowledge and vnderftanding. *Iere.3.* Such were Ezra amongft the Ifraelites, Epaphroditus at Philippos, Epaphras at Co-
loffos, Apollos at Corinth: fuch are many (thanks
be to God) in this land: therefore an ignorant minifter is a grieuous plague, for he cannot ftrengthē
the weake, heale the ficke, binde together the broken. *Ezech.34.*

The Popifh and Anabaptifticall fort haue done
great hurt in this land. This is as cleare as the funne:
the way to heale this fore, is to prouide fuch, as by
fouereigne plaifters and medicine out of the Lords
Eden may remoue this dangerous infection, and
plant in the peoples hearts the Lords holy religion.

Where teaching is not, the people are in a woful
cafe. Solomon faith, *Where prophecie* (that is, the ex-
pounding of Gods word) *is not, the people perifh.* *Pro-*
uerb.29. Almightie God faith, *My people perifh for*
want of knowledge. Hof.4. Our fauiour Chrift faith,
This is life eternall, that they might knowe thee, the onely
true God, and Iefus Chrift whom thou haft fent. Ioh.17.

Where found teachers are placed, thefe com-
modities are apparant. Firft, Almightie God is no-
tablie

tablie ferued. Secondly, the prince is duetifully o-
beyed. Thirdly, the enemie to religiō is either won
or defcried. Where the people are not taught,
thefe abfurdities doe followe : Firft, they cannot
ferue God, for they doe not knowe God. *Efay.19.*
Prius eft Deum fcire, confequens colere, Secondly, the
prince is not fo dutifullie obeyed : the rebellion in
the North, is a proofe of that. Laftly, the enemie
to religion cannot be wonne : for faith commeth
by hearing. *Rom.10.* nor fo eafily defcried : for the
holy word is a fearcher. *Hebr.4.*

All which loue the religion, haue and doe defire
a greater nomber of able teachers, that our church
may haue more beautie, our prince more honour,
our people more heauenly comfort. None miflike
this, but fuch as make Gods Church either a marke
to fhoote at. or a carkaffe to feede vpon. The one
forte are profeffed enemies : the other, graceleffe hypocrites. For they preferre myre
before pearles, earth before heauen,
and their filthie fwine before Iefus Chrift, as the Gerge-
fens did, *Mat.8.*

B.iiii.   4. THE

4. THE TEACHERS OF
Religion, muſt haue maintenance.

O ſhewe kindeneſſe to the Lordes houſe, is an excellent worke : ſo did Nehemias a courtier. To prouide maintenance for the teachers, is to ſhewe kindneſſe to the Lords houſe, *Nehem. 13. verſe 14.* Whatthen is their kindeneſſe, which ſell Church liuings as Iudas did Chriſt?The abominable ſale and marchandiſe of Church liuings is cried out againſt in Court, Citie, and Vniuerſities. *Propter abundantiam,* as one ſaid of late, *non poteſt, & propter impudentiam non vult celari :* that is, the polling and ſale of Church liuings is ſo common that it cannot, and ſo ſhameles that it will not be hidde.

To forſake the houſe of God, is a heinous ſinne: not to prouide for the teachers, is to forſake the houſe of God, *Nehem. 10.* and *13. Chap.* Howe greate then is their ſinne which robbe the Church and Churchmen? It is a groſſe ſinne to ſpoyle either the ſouldier or the merchãt aduenturer, which in their places are a ſingular defence to their countrey by ſea and land: therefore it is a heinous ſinne to robbe Churchmen, which (as Elias) are the Chariots and horſemen of the common wealth. *The weapons of our warrefare (ſaith the Apoſtle) are not carnal, but mighty through God, to caſt downe holdes, caſting downe the imaginations, and euery high thing that is exalted againſt the knowledge of God, and bringing into captiuitie euery thought to the obedience of Chriſt, and hauing ready the*

vengeance

vengeance against all disobedience.&c.2.Cor.10.

The repairing of Churches is to bee performed carefully: So was it in king Ioas time, therefore much more prouision for the teachers:the Prieftes maintenance in Ioas time, neither was nor might be abridged for repairing of the Churches:the reason of it is conteined in thefe wordes, *The money of the trefpaffe offering,and the money of the Sinne offring was not brought into the Lordes houfe : for it was the Priefts.2.Kings.12.*

Skilfull teachers doe plough the Lords field,and are the Lords,both mouth and hands to deliuer his bleffings and treafure vnto vs: therefore they ought to haue defence and maintenance,and not to wander as Michas Prieft did.*Iudg.17.* Students cannot liue of the ayre as the Chamelion doth. Church pollers fhut vp the kingdome of heauen before mē: for they themfelues goe not in, neither fuffer they them that would enter to come in : therefore the woe denounced by Chrift againft the Scribes and Pharifes,feazeth vpon them.*Matth.23.*

Ezechias the King of Iuda commanded that the Priefts and Leuites fhould haue maintenance, and that their wiues, children and families fhould bee prouided for.*2.Chron.31.verf.4,18.Thus did Hezekiah throughout all Iudah,and did well and vprightly,and truely before the Lord his God. And in all the works that he began for the feruice of the houfe of God,both in the Law and in the Commandements,to feeke his God,he did it with all his heart,and profpered. 2.Chron.31.verf.20,21.*

Diuers famous Princes haue had fome Churchmen to be of their honorable Councel: Iehoiada was in King Ioas Court.*2. Chron.24.* Zadok and A-

biathar,

biathar, in Dauid and Salomons Court, *2.Sam.20.*
1.King.4. Daniel in Darius Court.*Dan.6.*

It is Queene Elizabeths pleasure, that the worthiest men should bee aduaunced for the gouernement and seruice of the Church. That very meane choise hath bene made of diuers Churchmen, the land sees, feeles, and cries out of.

Question.

Whether such thinges as were giuen for the maintenance of idolatry, may, and ought to be conuerted to the seruice of God?

Answere.

They may, and ought. My reasons are:

If men should conuert them to their priuate vse, it might be iustly thought, that in abolishing superstition, priuate gaine is the marke which is shot at, and not the aduancing of Gods religion. *August. epist.154.*

When such things are conuerted, not to priuate, but common vses, or to the honour of God, that falleth out in them, which in men themselues, when of Church robbers and wicked men, they are conuerted to true religion. *August.epist.154.*

Eleazar the Priest tooke the brasen censers, which they that were burnt had offered, and made broad plates of them for a couering of the Altar. *Numb.16.*

The gold, siluer, the vessels of brasse and Iron in Iericho, were brought into the Lordes treasury. *Ios.6.*

Gedeon did offer vnto the Lorde, a bullocke which had bin fed for Baals seruice, and did vse the wood of the groue adioyning. *Iudg.6.*

If

If such thinges as were giuen to the maintenance of Poperie, may not be conuerted to the seruice of God, then pull downe Churches and Vni-
uersities, take away their landes &c. And let A-
theisme be in steade of Gods religion, and Macci-
auell in the place of the new Testament.

5. ## ALMIGHTIE GOD
*blesseth those kingdomes with peace, which
promote and embrace his religion.*

He holy ghost setteth out in liuely
colours, the cósequents of teaching
and embracing the Lordes religion.
*They shall breake their swordes into
mattockes, and their speares into
siethes: they shall sit euery man vnder his vine, and figge
tree without feare of the enemie.* Mich.4. The prophet Esay singeth the same song: *The Wolfe shall
dwell with the Lambe: The Leoparde shall lie with the
kidde, the Cowe and the Beare shall feede together.
Esay.11.* That is, wicked men which in cruell af-
fections resemble the Wolfe, the Leoparde, the
Beare, shall cast off the chaine of pride, and the garment of crueltie, and shall goe hand in hand with
the godlie, who for their innocencie are compa-
red to the Lambe, the Cowe, the Kidde. The reason is: *For the earth shall be filled with the knowledge of
the Lorde. Esay.11.*
The Egyptians and Assyrians were deadly enemies: they denied traffique one to an other, and all
passages were shut vp betweene Egypt and Assyria.

Esay

Efay defcribing a great alterationof minds in them of Egypt and Affyria, fayth, that *There fhall be a path from Egypt to Affur : and Affur fhall come into Egypt, and Egypt into Affur.* The reafon of their agreement, is fet downe in thefe words: *The Egyptians fhall worfhip (the Lord) with Affur. Efay 19.*

Where idolatrie is aduanced , no peace can bee looked for. *They chofe newe gods,* faith Deborah, *Then was warre in the gates. Iudg. 5. The Ifraelites for a long time were without the true God, without Prieft to teach : In that time ,* faith the Prophet Azariah, *there was no peace : for nation was deftroyed of nation ,and citie of citie. 2. Chron. 15.* The Reubenites, Gadites, and halfe tribe of Manaffeh, *tranfgreffed againft the God of their fathers,and went a whoring after the gods of the people of the lande , whome God had deftroyed before them : Tha God of Ifrael ftirred vp the fpirit of the kings of Affyria, who caryed them away captiue,&c.1. Chron. 5.* Iehoram the king of Iuda, did forfake the Lorde God of his fathers : the confequents were : *Edom, Libnah, rebelled : the Lorde ftirred vp againft Iehoram , the fpirit of the Philiftines & Arabians.2.Chron.21.* King Ahaz was a notable idolater : *He facrificed to the gods of Damafcus : the Edomites, and Philiftines inuaded the cities of Iuda,and preuailed :* Yea, the king of Affyria, whofe helpe Ahaz defired, and accounted greatly of, *did trouble and not ftrengthen him. 2. Chron.28.* Iehoiakim the king of Iuda, did euill in the fight of the Lorde his God : *The king of Babel came vp againft him, and bound him with chaines to carie him to Babel.2.Chron.36.*

They which diffent in religion, cannot bee knit faft together. The Samaritanes and Iewes differed in religion : they contended about the Temple. *Ioh.4.*

Ioh.4. The ſtirre betweene them was very great.
Some in the Apoſtles times after Chriſts aſcenſiõ,
vrged circumciſion as neceſſary vnto ſaluation: o-
ther condemned it as an abſurd & groſſe error. The
ſtirre was great in the Churches of Antiochia and
Galatia. Arius erred blaſphemouſly about the god-
head of Chriſt: Alexander the biſhop of Alexandria, both miſliked & condemned his filthy hereſie.
Socrat.lib.1.ca.6. There was hotte ſtirre in the church
of Alexandria. The Lordes arke, and the Philiſtines
Dagon: the Epheſians Diana, and Pauls preaching:
Poperie, and the Goſpell cannot ſtand together.

Aſa was a religous Prince: he ſuppreſſed idolatrie and planted Gods religion. *The kingdome was
quiet before him, and hee vanquiſhed the Ethiopians.2.
Chron.14.& 15.Chap.*

Ioſaphat was a zealous promoter of the Lords religion. Almightie God crowned him with this bleſſing: *The feare of the Lorde fell vpon all the kingdomes
of the lande that were round about Iudah, and they fought
not againſt Ioſaphat: the Philiſtines brought to Ioſaphat
giftes and tribute ſiluer: the Arabians brought him flockes
both of rammes and goates.2.Chron.17.*

Vzziah the King of Iuda, *proſpered ſo long as hee
ſought the Lord. Almightie God helped him againſt the
Philiſtines and Arabians: the Ammonites gaue him
tribute, and his name was famous euen vnto Egypt.2.
Chron.26.*

Ezechias was a carefull aduancer of Gods religion. *The land had great quietneſſe, and was notably deliuered from the Aſſirians. 2.Chron.32.*

Queene Elizabeth hath planted the Lords religion. Popes; Gregory, Pius, Sixtus, haue curſed her
C.iii.   Maieſtie:

Maieſtie:the Popiſh enemies hauebene & are ma-
liciouſly bent againſt her,& this land,as Sennache-
rib &Rabſakeh againſt Ezechias and Ieruſalem: but
God hath bleſſed,and miraculouſly preſerued her
Highnes and Dominions,as he did Ezechias & Ie-
ruſalem:the greateſt enemies of the Engliſh natiõ,
are the ſinnes of the Engliſh nation: but if we deſire
and obtaine pardon for our ſinnes at Gods hands,
& ſhal ſerue our God,& ſanctifie his Sabboth more
carefully then we haue done,the Lord wil goe forth
with our armies, our captaines and ſouldiers ſhall
amaze and vanquiſh our Popiſh enemies, as *Gedeon*
did the *Madianites*, *Iephthe* the *Ammonites*,and *Dauid* the *Philiſtines*: and our gracious God will couer
both Prince & people with the ſhield of his Iuſtice,
and defend vs with the ſworde of his Iudgement.

Obiection.

When the Goſpell is preached, ſtirres doe
grow: that appeared in Ieruſalem. *Act.7.* in Iconi-
um.*Act.14.*in Rome.*Act.28.*

Anſwere.

I grant that ſtirres appeare ſometimes, when
Gods trueth is deliuered : the fault is not in the
ſeede,but in the ground.It was not Elias that troubled Iſrael,but Achab and his fathers houſe, which
forſooke the Lords commandements, & followed
Baal.*1.King.18.* The holy preaching reſembles medicine,daylight,and the heate of the ſunne. It is
not the medicine,but euil humors which diſtemper
the body: varietie of colours are not made, but diſ-
cerned by the day light. The heate of the ſunne is
not the cauſe,but the deſcrier of the ſtinke of a car-
rion.

6. THE

6. THE CHILDE OF

G O D is not polluted, though hee bee pre-
fent at, and partaker of the publique prayers,
Sacraments, &c.at fuch time, as wicked men
are prefent at, and partakers of them.

N the Prophets time, there were many & groffe corruptions at Ierufalem.
The magiftrates, Priefts and people
were greatly difordered: The Lordes
religion was partly contemned, and
partly defiled. Did the holy Prophets feuer them
felues from them of Ierufalem in Salomons temple? Did they builde newe, either Churches to af-
femble in, or Altars to facrifice vpon? It is certaine,
they did not, and yet they were not polluted.

Our Sauiour Chrift was prefented to the Lord
in Ierufalem. An oblation was giuen. *Luk.2.22.* Hee
was afterwards partaker of the Sacrifices in Salomons temple, with the Scribes, Pharifes, & vngra-
tious people of Ierufalem. My reafons are: Firft,
Chrift was fubiect to the law. *Gal.4.4.* One branch of
the Law was, to be partaker of the Sacrifices in Salomons temple. Secondly, Chrift in the dialogue
with the woman of Samaria, fpeaking of himfelfe,
and the Iewes, vfeth thefe wordes: *We worfhip that*
which we knowe. Ioh.4.22. Vnder the worde (*wor-*
fhip) are contained the facrifices. *Calu. contra A-*
nabapt.

The Churches of Corinth and Galatia, had many and groffe fores in them. Saint Paul, I confeffe,
deales very roundly with them: yet hee doth not,

either licenfe, or cal vpon Gods feruants in Corinth and Galatia , to feuer themfelues from the affemblies. If to be prefent in the affemblie had brought pollution , the Apoftle woulde not haue failed in this Chriftian dutie.

Let a man examine himfelfe. *1.Cor, 11.28.* The Apoftle doeth not fay , Let euery man examine the reft of the communicants : which no doubt hee would haue giuen in charge , if the lewdneffe of others did pollute Gods feruants.

He that eateth and drinketh vnworthily , eateth and drinketh iudgement to himfelfe. *1.Cor.11.29.* Saint Paul faith *(to himfelfe)* not to others.

The Apoftles receiued the Lords fupper with Iudas. *Aug. contra Lit. Petil. lib. 2. cap. 11. & 23. & lib. 3. cap. 106.* But they were not partakers of Iudas theft. *Aug. contra Crefc. Gram. lib. 4. cap. 26.* or Iudas treafon. *Acceditur ad vitium corruptionis, vitio confenfionis. Aug. contra Don. poft Coll. lib.* That is, to confent to vice, is to bee corrupted with vice. That Iudas was a theefe, Saint Iohn reporteth. *Ioh. 12. verf. 6.* That the Apoftles did knowe before the partaking of the holy fupper , that Iudas fhould betray Chrift, appeareth manifeftly in the Euangelift Matthewe. *Matt. 26. verf. 21,23,25.*

The moft famous men, before, and in our time, are of my fide. *Auguftine* in his writings againft *Petilian, Parmeniä, Crefconius,* the Donatifts: and *Caluin* in his treatife againft the Anabaptiftes, are very peremptory in this Argument. None can , or wil miflike it, vnleffe they be alreadie, or meane to bee Donatiftes, or Anabaptiftes,

Obiection.

Obiection.

The Apoſtle commaundes vs to withdrawe our ſelues from euery brother that walketh inordinately. *2. Theſſ.3.6.*

Anſwere.

We muſt withdrawe our ſelues, *Quoad priuatam conſuetudinem, non quoad publicam communionem:* that is, touching priuate conuerſation, not touching publike partaking of the worde and Sacraments. *Caluin* is of this Iudgement, in his treatiſe againſt the Anabaptiſtes.

If any ſhall gather of this I haue ſet downe, that I am content to admit notorious ſinners to the holy table, he doth me great wrong, and is refuted in my treatiſe of the Sacraments, where I vſe theſe wordes: It is a great ſinne for a knowen wicked man, either to miniſter the Lordes ſupper, or to preſent himſelfe to the holy communion : and ſuch lewdnes muſt bee ſeuerelie puniſhed, by them in whoſe handes it is to redreſſe it. But if this groſſe ſinne be practiſed, and no medicine vſed to cure it, the godly muſt content them ſelues with griefe for theſe enormities, and remember that the Sacrament ſealeth vp Gods ſweete promiſes to them, which the wicked ſort at no hand are partakers of.

D.i. 7. THEY

7. THEY WHICH WERE
baptized in the Popiſh Church by Popiſh Prieſtes, receiued true Baptiſme, touching the ſubſtance of Baptiſme.

He Popiſh prieſtes doe retaine the eſſential forme of Chriſts baptiſme, that is, they doe baptiſe in the name, not of Pope or idoles, but of the holy Trinitie: therefore it is not mans, but Gods baptiſme, which is deliuered by them. If it be Gods baptiſme, I am ſure it is true baptiſme, Maiſter *Caluin* calleth them *Catabaptiſtes*, which deny that wee are rightly baptized in the Popiſh Church. *Inſtitut. lib. 4. cap. 15. Sect. 16.*

Obiection.

The Popiſh prieſtes haue no lawfull calling: therefore, it is no true baptiſme which is deliuered by them.

Anſwere.

The Argument followes not. I confeſſe that the Popiſh prieſts haue no lawful calling: yet, they haue a calling, though a faultie one. They which are not lawfully called vnto the miniſtery, and yet ſit in the chaire of the miniſterie, are to bee accounted in an other place then they which haue no calling. *Caiphas* was not in deede the lawfull high prieſt: for he entred by money, & the prieſthood in his time was rent in peeces: yet, becauſe he ſate in the high prieſts chaire, he was accounted the high prieſt. A faultie vocation may hurt him that vſurpes an office, but it doth not defile thoſe things which are done by that partie.

This

This is mafter Bezaes Iudgement in his 141. queftion.

Ifany fhall gather of this, that I allowe the Popifh priefthood,he deferues rather a Cenfor, then Confuter: for I confeffe that *Sacerdotium papifticum eft facrilegium:* that is,that the Popifh priefthood is *Sacriledge.*

8. THEY ARE THE SAcraments of *Baptifme and the holy Supper, which are deliuered in the Church of England, by vnpreaching minifters.*

F fuch as were baptized in the popifh Church, receiued true baptifme, I truft they are rightly baptized in the Church of England,which are baptized by vnpreaching minifters.

If fuch as were baptized by popifh priefts in the popifh Church, and by vnpreaching minifters in the Church of England, receiued no facrament, many groffe abfurdities would followe. Firft,very many are vnbaptized: and if they bee vnbaptized, they finne grieuoufly,in not prefenting themfelues to the holy Sacrament. Secondly, a great number haue finned groffely in partaking the holy fupper. My reafon is : None vncircumcifed might eate the Paffeouer. *Exodus 12.verfe 48.* therefore none vnbaptized may receiue the holy fupper. Thirdly, many excellent men haue vfurped the preachers office. My reafon is : It is vnlawfull for any man to bee a publique teacher in the vifible

Church,

Church,which is not by baptifme graft into, and
fo become a member of the vifible Church.Our Sauiour Chrift was baptized of Iohn in Iordane,be-
fore hee preached. *Matth. 3.and 4. Chap.* The Apoftle Paul was baptized of Ananias in Damafcus,
before hee preached. *Act.9.*

The vnpreaching Minifters doe adde the worde
vnto the Element in the adminiftration of Baptifme: therefore it is the Sacramēt of Baptifme which
is deliuered by them. *Accedit verbum ad elementum,
& fit Sacramentum. Aug.Tract.80. in Iohan.* that is,
The worde is added to the Element,and it becoms
a Sacrament.By *(worde)* in Baptifme, is vnderftanded the word of Inftitution,which is, to Baptize in
the name of the father, the fonne, and the holy
Ghoft,&c. Of this iudgement are *Beza confeff.Cap.4.
Art.47.* and *Mufculus de fig.Sacram.Art.4.*

Obiection.

Chrift fayde to his Apoftles, *Goe and teach all
nations,baptizing &c. Matth.28.verf.19.* therefore, if
the word preached, be not added to the Element,
it is no Sacrament of Baptifme.

Anfwere.

The argument is very weake. I confeffe, that
Chrift commanded his Apoftles,firft to teach fuch
as were of yeeres and alients from his religion, and
then to baptize them.If the Gentiles had not bene
firft taught,they would not haue offered thē felues,
nor the Apoftles haue admitted them to the holy
Sacrament of baptifme.If any will conclude of this
place in Saint Mathewe, that none whatfoeuer
may bee admitted to baptifme before they bee
taught,they fhut our infants from the holy Sacrament,

ment,and therefore are Catabaptiſts.

The vnpreaching miniſters doe adde *(verbum ædificans)* that is,an edifying worde,to the Elements in the adminiſtration of the holy ſupper, therefore &c.

That there is *verbum ædificans*,I proue it thus.

The ſumme of Chriſtes ſermon in the Inſtitution & adminiſtration of the holy ſupper by himſelfe, is the word of Inſtitution in the adminiſtration of the holy Supper in the Church of England : therefore,vnleſſe we wil denie the ſumme of Chriſts Sermon,to be an edifying word,(which no learned mã wil deny)we muſt confeſſe,that we haue *verbum ædificans* in the adminiſtration of the holy ſupper with vs.

If any will conclude of this, that I miſlike preaching before the adminiſtration of the Sacrament, he doth me great wrong.

Obiection.

Vnpreaching miniſters are not apt to teach: therefore they are no Sacraments which are deliuered by them.

Anſwere.

The argument followes not.My reaſon is,Many Iewiſh Prieſtes were both ignorant and diſſolute in Eſay and Chriſts time.*Eſay 28. verſ.7. Matth. 9.verſ. 36.* But the Sacrifices offered, and the Sacraments reached by them, were both Sacrifices and Sacraments: otherwiſe,the Prophets which were at Ieruſalem,when the Iewiſh Church was full of corruption, woulde not haue bene preſent at, and partakers of the Sacrifices in Salomons Temple.*Calu. Inſtitut.lib.4.cap.1.ſect.18,19.*

D.iii.   *Obiection.*

Obiection.

Ignorant minifters are not apt to teach : therefore no minifters,and confequently,they are no Sacraments which are deliuered by them.

Anfwere.

The argument followes not, I grant that it is of the fubftance of a lawful & good minifter of God to be apt to teach : but it is not of the effence of a Minifter fimply : for which it is fufficient to haue the Churches calling. This appeareth clearely in the Magiftrate. The holy Ghoft requireth that none fhoulde bee chofen a Magiftrate, vnleffe he were a man of courage, fearing God, dealing truely,and hating couetoufneffe. *Exodus. 18. verfe 21.* When fuch are aduanced as defile their handes, either with filthie bribes, as *Felix* did, or with barbarous crueltie , as *Abimelech* and *Herode* did, fhall we fay that they are no Magiftrates ? I confeffe,they are not fingled out by the electors according to Almightie Gods direction in his holy Bible : but they are Magiftrates notwithftanding, and we are commanded by the Lord to perfourme all duetie vnto them, *Saluo officio,* that is, our duetie being referued to the higheft Magiftrate, which is God himfelfe.

If any fhall gather of this I haue fet downe, that I vndertake the defence of Ignorant minifters : my anfwere is,that my writings and fermons, are not Aiax fhielde to couer them,but the Lords fworde to cutte them. I confeffe freely,that I am very farre from opening either the Church doore to ignorant Minifters , or the Pulpit doore to vnfkilfull preachers: which vnfkilfull preachers giue Gods

religion

religion a greater blowe then the ignorant Minifters: for in fteade of deuiding the worde of trueth
aright, they fpeake at al aduentures, yet very boldely: and as vnfkilfull Apothecaries, deliuer *quid pro
quo*, chaffe for wheate, and ftrange fancies for Gods
holy trueth. By fuch abfurde fellowes, many Churches and excellent men in this lande haue beene
greatly difquieted, and the good courfe of religion
hath beene greatly hindered. The caufe of this fore,
is intollerable pride, and groffe ignorance in thefe
bad companions, and want of care in the Magiftrates.

If any fhall aske mee what the true caufes are,
why fo many vnfitte men are the Churches Minifters: I anfwere, either great want of iudgement, or
great corruption in fuch, which doe ordeine and
preferre them. The finne of thefe men is very great:
for they difhonour Almightie God, and do grofly
abufe the people of the land. This difeafe will bee
healed, when the Churches maintenance is not difpofed of by them which haue the golden
dropfie, but is freely giuen to worthie and
painefull ftudents, which will neither fifh with the filuer hooke,
nor open the Church
doore with a fil-
uer key.

9. THE GODLY ARE
not polluted which receiue the Sacrament at the handes of an vnpreaching Minister.

THE Sacramentes are Gods ordinance: the Ministers ignorance cannot peruert the nature of Gods ordinance.

A Sacrament can neuer be without promise of saluation : therefore, the worthy partaker of the Sacrament receiues a blessing: if a blessing, then no pollution. That he receiues a blessing, the Apostle teacheth vs : *We are buried with Christ (saith S. Paul) by baptisme into his death, &c. Rom.6. verse 4. The cuppe of blessing which we blesse, is it not the communion of the blood of Christ? The bread which wee breake, is it not the communion of the body of Christ? 1. Cor.11.verse 16.*

The parents of Christ went to Ierusalem euery yere at the feast of the Passeouer, *Luk.2.vers.41.* their going to Ierusalem, was to testifie their religion, & to be partakers of the sacrifices. There were at that time in Salomons Temple manifold corruptions, the high Priesthood was solde for money, many of the Iewish Priests were ignorant, yet Ioseph & the virgine Mary were not polluted. *Calu. Luc.2.verf.41.*

The godly which receiue the holy Supper of an vnpreaching Minister, are not partakers of the Ministers vnworthinesse, but of the holy Sacrament, which is a pillar of our faith: therefore the vnworthinesse of the Minister doth not defile the Communicat. *Alterius, siue Pastoris, siue priuati indignitate,*
non

*non læditur pia conſcientia,&c.Calu.Inſtitut. lib.4.cap.1.
Sect. 19.*that is, A godly conſcience is not hurt by
the vnworthineſſe of an other,either Paſtor, or priuate man : neither are the myſteries leſſe pure and
healthfull to a holy man , becauſe they are then
handled of ſuch as be impure. *Ille qui accipit, ſi homo
bonus ab homine malo,ſi fidelis à perfido,ſi pius ab impio:
pernicioſum erit danti, non accipienti. Illud quippe ſanctum male vtentem iudicat, bene accipientem ſanctificat.
Aug.contra Creſc.gram.lib.2.cap.28.*that is, he which
receiueth,if a good of an euill man, if a faithfull of
a faithleſſe man,if a godly of a wicked man , it will
be hurtful to the giuer,not to the receiuer : for that
holy thing(he meaneth the ſacrament) doth iudge
him which vſeth it ill,but doeth ſanctifie him which
receiueth it well.

Circumciſion was one of the Lords Sacraments
in the Iewiſh Church. The Iewes which were circumciſed of impure prieſtes,and Apoſtates, receiued no hurt: therefore no pollution. *Calu. Inſtitut.
lib.4.cap.15.Sect.16.* The Sacraments neither are,
nor can be the worſe for the ignorance or vnworthineſſe : or better for the learning or worthineſſe
of any man whatſoeuer. Whoſoeuer thinketh o-
therwiſe, is a Donatiſt.

Touching this point of the Sacrament , I reſt
wholy in Auguſtines iudgement : his wordes are
theſe.*Ego dico,melius per bonū miniſtrū quàm per malū
diſpenſari ſacramenta diuina: verùm hoc propter ipſum
miniſtrum melius eſt,vt eis rebus quas miniſtrat, vita &
moribus congruat,non propter illum, qui etiam ſi incurrerit in miniſtrum malum diſpenſantem veritatem,ſecu-
ritatem accipit à domino ſuo monente ac dicente : Quæ*

dicunt

dicunt facite, quæ autem faciunt, nolite facere : dicunt enim, & non faciunt. Addo etiam ad hoc eſſe melius, vt ille cui miniſtratur, miniſtri boni probitatem ac ſanĉti-tatem diligendo faciliùs imitetur : Sed non ideo veriora & ſanĉtiora ſunt quæ miniſtrantur ; quia per meliorem miniſtrantur. Illa namque per ſeipſa vera & ſanĉta ſunt, propter Deum verum & ſanĉtum cuius ſunt, & ideo fieri poteſt vt accedens ad ſocietatem populi Dei, alium inueniat à quo facilè baptizetur, alium eligat quem ſalubriter imitetur. Certus eſt enim ſanĉtum eſſe Sacramentum Chriſti, etiamſi per minùs ſanĉtum, vel non ſanĉtum hominem miniſtratum eſt, ſe autem eiuſ-dem ipſius ſacramenti ſanĉtitate puniri, ſi indignè acce-perit, ſi malè vſus fuerit, ſi ei non conuenienter & con-gruè vixerit. Auguſt. contra Creſc. Gram. lib. 4. cap. 20.

The ſumme of Auguſtines wordes is, that the Sacra-ment is adminiſtred better by a good, then by a bad Miniſter: yet that the Sacraments of themſelues are true and holy, &c. by what miniſter ſo euer they be deliuered, &c. If any ſhall aske mee whether it be lawful to omit the partaking of the holy Sacrament in ſuch Churches ouer which ignorant miniſters are ſet, and to preſent our ſelues and our infants to the holy Sacrament in other Churches : my an-ſwere is, that I referre them to the Magiſtrate and Gouernours of our Churches, &c.

Obieĉtion.

By whome a thing ought not to be deliuered, by another it ought not to bee receiued: but ignorant miniſters ought not to deliuer the Sacraments, therefore, &c.

Anſwere.

The Maior is falſe. My reaſon is: An euill man ought

ought not to deliuer the worde of God, but wee ought to receiue it. An euill man ought not to giue almes, but a poore man may receiue it. An abſurde miniſter ought not to deliuer the Sacrament, but they are not polluted which receiue it.

Obiection.

They, of whoſe miniſterie there is a Nullitie before God, although they haue an outwarde calling, ought not to bee accompted miniſters: therefore not to bee communicated with. *I.Penry.pag. 43,44.*

Anſwere.

I denie your Antecedent. My reaſons are: Firſt, there was a Nullitie before God of Caiphas Prieſthoode: for hee entred by money, and the Prieſthood was deuided betweene him and Annas, againſt the Lords order. *Calu. Luc.3.* yet Caiphas is called the high Prieſt, by the Euangeliſts. *Mat.26. Ioh.18.* Secondly, there was a Nullitie before God, of the miniſterie of ſome in Philippos, which preached Chriſt of contention, and to adde more affliction to Pauls bandes. *Philip.Chap.1.verſe 15,16.* But theſe are accompted miniſters by the Apoſtle. *verſ. 15,18.* If any ſhall deny that there was a Nullitie before God of their miniſterie, I prooue it thus: They had not an inward calling. *M.Penry* ſaith, that an inward calling is contained in the ſufficiécie of gifts, and willingneſſe to practiſe them. *pag.45.* If *M.Penry* meane the practiſe of giftes to Gods glory, I ſay, Amen, vnto it. I confeſſe that they of Philippos had giftes in ſome meaſure, but they had not willingneſſe to practiſe thoſe giftes to Gods glorie: which willingneſſe &c. is one of the neceſſarie

E.ii. branches

branches of an inward calling. That they of Philippos had not this willingneſſe, &c. it is manifeſt:
for they ſought themſelues, and practiſed their gifts
wholy to increaſe the Apoſtles affliction. Laſtly, if
your Antecedent be true, what ſay you to this propoſition ? They, of whoſe Magiſtracie there is a
Nullitie before God, though they haue an outward
calling, ought not to bee accompted Magiſtrates.
Doe you not thinke this propoſition to bee very
dangerous ? I could preſſe and followe this very
farre, but I abſtaine of purpoſe.

Obiection.

The Sacrament may not bee receiued at his
handes which wanteth outward calling : Therefore not at his handes, who is deſtitute of the inward graces. *I.Penry.pag.46.*

Anſwere.

Your Antecedent is true, and maketh againſt
the Anabaptiſts. I denie your Argument. My reaſon is : *Omnia Sacramenta, cùm obſint indignè tractantibus, proſunt tamen per eos dignè ſumentibus. Auguſt.
contra epiſt.Parmen. lib. 2. cap. 10.* That is, All Sacraments, though they hurt ſuch as doe handle them
vnworthily, yet they profit ſuch as doe worthily
receiue them at their handes.

Obiection.

We haue no warrant to receiue an extraordinarie Sacrament : But that which is adminiſtred by
ignorant miniſters, is an extraordinary Sacrament,
if it be any : Therefore, we haue no warrant to receiue it. *I.Penry.pag.49.*

Anſwere.

I denie your Minor, and doe adde this : Firſt,
that

that it 'is a Sacrament by your owne confeſſion,
*pag.50,51.*which is adminiſtred by ignorant miniſters. Secondly,that it is no extraordinarie Sacrament,which is deliuered by them, vnleſſe you will
call Baptiſme and the holy Supper, extraordinarie
Sacraments.

If any will conclude of theſe my anſweres , that
I miſlike *M.Penryes* deſire of a learned Miniſterie in
Wales,he takes vp that which I neuer let fall: for I
deſire with all my heart, and the Lorde for his
Chriſts fake grant it,that not onely Wales may be
furniſhed with worthy gouernours and paſtours,
but all other partes of her Maieſties Dominions,
that Gods graces may be more and more multiplied vpon vs and our poſteritie, and his holy hand
watch ouer vs.

10 THE CHVRCH OF
England is the viſible Church of Chriſt.

HE Church of Galatia which erred
in a fundamentall point of doctrine,
is called the Church of God, *Gal.1.*
therefore,the Church of England,
which erreth not in any fundamen-
tall point of doctrine,is the Church of Chriſt.That
the Church of Galatia erred in a fundamentall
point of doctrine, it is manifeſt : for they ioyned
Circumciſion and Chriſt together.If any do thinke
that the Church of England doe hold an errour in
any fundamentall point of doctrine, let him ſet
downe the particular.

E.iii.   The

The Church of England hath Chrift for her head and foundation: for fhee receiueth and reuerenceth the Canonicall Scriptures, and confeffeth Chriftes righteoufneffe to be hers, and that faluation is compaffed by Chrift alone, with whofe grace nothing may bee matched. *Chriftus aut totus aut nullus. Gratia Dei aut tota fufcipitur, aut tota reijcitur. Gratia nullo modo effet gratia,nifi effet omni modo gratuita.*

That the preaching of the holy worde and adminiftration of the Sacraments are the effentiall markes of the Church of Chrift, I haue proued in my Treatife of the Church, to which booke I referre you: but thefe effentiall markes of the Church, are in the Church of England: therefore,&c.

Obiection.

The difcipline vfed in the Primitiue Church, is not in the Church of Englād: therefore the church of England is not the Church of Chrift.

Anfwere.

I denie the Argument. My reafons are: Firft, *S.Luke* fetting out the extraordinary bleffing which God gaue to Peters fermō in Ierufalem, hath thefe wordes: *Then they that gladly receiued his worde, were baptized : and the fame day,there were added (to the Church)about three thoufand foules. And they continued in the Apoftles doctrine, and fellowfhip, and breaking of bread,and prayers.Acts. 2.41,42.*No man endued with Gods fpirit,wil denie that this affembly which was baptifed & continued in the Apoftles doctrine,&c. was the Church of God,and yet no Deacons were at that time chofē,or Confiftories of Seniors erected.

ted. Secondly, they which doe vrge the difcipline
moft earneftly, doe confeffe that the difcipline is
not an effentiall part of the Church. Their reafon
is : The difcipline refembles the wall of a Citie, and
hedge or ditch of a Vineyarde. It is a Citie, though
the wall bee wanting : it is a Vineyarde, though
hedge or ditch be wanting, Laftly, I woulde gladly
knowe, whether it bee either poffible, or fafe, to
plant that difcipline in this lande, before that Gods
holy Trueth be foundly both taught and receiued,
and that there be fit Churchmen and people to execute the difcipline.

Obiection.

The Minifters in England are not chofen by the
Parifhes ouer which they are fet : therefore they
are no minifters, and confequently there is no adminiftration of the worde or Sacraments, no wor-
fhippe of God, nor vifible Church in England, as
fome Anabaptifts haue giuen out of late.

Anfwere.

I denie the Argument. My reafon is : if this Argument of theirs were good, thefe abfurdities
would follow. Firft, that Gods Church is neceffarily tyed in all places and times to one forme in the
externall calling of the minifters. Secondly, that
the excellent affemblie in the Primitiue Church,
Actes 2.verfe 41,42. was not the Church of God : for
at that time, the Minifters were not elected by the
Prefbitery & people. Thirdly, that the worthieft
Preachers in this land, are no Minifters. Laftly, that
very many parts of England are like to haue no teachers, becaufe they are vtterly vnfit to make choife
of their Paftours. If it be faide that fome Bifhops in

E.iiii.   ordeining

ordeyning, and fome Patrones in prefenting ignorant Minifters, haue erred as grofly as any Parifh
can: my anfwere is, that I neither dare, nor will
defend fuch, either Bifhops or Patrons: I doe rather exhort them to vnfeyned repentance:
for this great finne of theirs hath, and
doth crie very loude for fome notable vengeance.

Cipri. de vnitate Ecclefiæ.

*Hæreſes (Diabolus) inuenit & ſchiſmata, quibus ſubuerteret fidem, ve-
ritatem corrumperet, ſcinderet vnitatem. Quos detinere non poteſt in viæ
veteris cæcitate, circumſcribit & decipit noui itineris errore. Rapit de ipſa
Eccleſia homines, & dum ſibi appropinquaſſe iam lumini, atq̃, euaſiſſe ſæ-
culi noctem videntur, alias neſcientibus tenebras rurſus infundit, &c.*

A

DEFENCE OF SVCH

POINTS IN R. SOMES

LAST TREATISE, AS

M. P ᴇ ɴ ʀ ʏ hath dealt
againſt:

And a refutation of many Anabaptiſti-
cal,blaſphemous and Popiſh abſurdities,tou=
ching Magiſtracie,Miniſterie,Church,Scrip-
ture and Baptiſme,&c.conteined in
M.Penryes treatiſe,&c.

By R. S ᴏ ᴍ ᴇ Doctour
of Diuinitie.

R ᴏ ᴍ. chap.16. verſ.17.18.
I beſeech you brethren,marke them diligently which cauſe diui-
ſion and offences, contrary to the doctrine which yee haue
learned,and auoyde them.
For they that are ſuch, ſerue not the Lord Ieſus Chriſt,but their
owne bellies, and with faire ſpeach and flattering decciue
the hearts of the ſimple.

Imprinted at London by G.B. Deputie to Chri-
ſtopher Barker, Printer to the Queenes moſt
excellent Maieſtie. 1588.

F.

To The Reader.

I *Did publish a short Treatise in May last. It hath pleased one M.* Penry *to examine part of it, and (as an other* Aristarchus*) to censure it. His booke was sent me. I haue viewed it, and doe finde strange things in it. Aduise was giuen me, not to vouchsafe an answere, because M.* Penry *is very ignorant, and his Treatise very sillie and corrupt stuffe. I considered waightely of it, but resolued to take some paines. The reasons which induced me, are: First, S.* Paul *vouchsafed in Gods cause to deale with* Demetrius *the siluer, and* Alexander *the copper smith. The Prophet* Ezechiel *in the like cause, did set himselfe against certaine wicked women &c.* Ezech. 13. *Secondly, many haue beene mislead by his absurd fancies. To cure these, if God will, and to stay other, my labour is not amisse. Lastly, I am personally both charged and chalenged by him: therefore it became me to take pen in hand. M.* Penries *booke is a fardle of grosse errours. None accompt of it, but such as are of the fantasticall crewe: men extremely both proude and ignorant. He hath as many learned men of his side, as* H. N. *the prince of the familie of Loue had of his: that is, neuer a one: therefore a little Arithmetique will serue to number them. If it had pleased him to haue considered of, and rested in the iudgement and direction of very famous men and Churches, he had not swarued from Gods booke, he had sailed by a sure compasse, he had not broched such fancies, as Gods Church with one voyce condemneth.* Nestorius *was an absurd heretike: he had some sparkles of eloquence by nature: hee was in his owne opinion learned, but in deede very ignorant: his pride was such, that he vouchsafed not to reade any interpreters.* Socrat. lib. 7. cap. 32. *I assure my selfe, that M.* Penry *is very farre from* Nestorius *heresie: I would he were as cleare of pride and contempt of writers.* Caluine, Beza, &c. *men of excellent learning, are cast off by him, euen in those waighty causes, wherein they shake hands with all the Churches of God. I doe not belie him, I charge him iustly: it shall appeare so by Gods grace in this Treatise. The question betweene him and me, is not whether ignorant men may either enter into, or continue in the holy ministerie: for, my resolution is negatiue, that is, that they ought*

F.ij   not:

To the Reader.

not : *but the question is, whether such as were and are baptized by Popish priests and ignorant ministers, haue and doe receiue a Sacrament: and whether the godly communicant is polluted by receiuing the Sacrament at the hands of vnpreaching ministers. The most famous men and Churches, are peremptorie for me, and against him. Yea,* M. Penry *himselfe ioyneth with me in many partes of his Treatise : in some other partes, I confesse, he sings an other song, absurde for matter, and out of tune for manner. This inconstancie of his proceedes from a vaine humour, which as a whirle-winde; doeth strangely carrie and ouer-carrie him. It is not in my handes to heale him : if it were, I woulde with all my heart. I will pray vnto God to cure him.* Cathedram in cœlo habet, qui corda docet. *All that I desire of the godly Reader,is,that he wil reade my Treatise before he giue sentence.Otherwise,I may iustly charge him,to bring not* iudicium,*but* præiudicium,*that is,to be very partiall. Let him,in Gods Name,compare my arguments and answeres with my aduersaries, and weigh them in equall balance : if hee doeth not see clearely, and feele sensibly his grosse errors & Anabaptisticall fancies,his eyes are dimme,his fingers are benummed.That he may haue present and speedie viewe of the pearles in his booke,I haue set downe in a Table, diuers strange particulers.If they seeme harsh and rough-hewen,blame* M.Penry: *for they come out of his forge. Yea,I dare be bolde to say,that if the Spiders webbe bee good cloth, and the Cockatrice egges holsome meate,then such points as I refute in this Treatise, are very excellent Diuinitie. I am not alone of this iudgement: the worthiest Diuines in this land iumpe with me, and do mislike and condemne his absurdities. It pleased God to assist mee graciously in the paines I haue taken: I thanke his Maiestie very humbly for it: I doubt not, but that he will giue a blessing vnto it. The Lord giue vs grace to see and know our ignorance,to be truely humble, to grow in godly knowledge,and not in Anabaptistical and blasphemous fancies.* London.
*Septemb.*19. *1588.*

Necessaria ignoramus,quia non necessaria discimus.

A TABLE

A TABLE OF SOME PRIN-
cipall particulers, conteined in this treatife.

A*Lmightie God neuer called any to bee Ma-
giſtrates, but hee furniſhed them accordingly.*   *Chap.3.pag.59.60.61.*
*Magiſtracie is Gods ordinance, not a deuiſe
of man.*   *Chap.13.page 136.137.*
The reading of the holy Scriptures, doeth edifie.   Chap.4.
pag.62.63.64.
The Scripture is of credit in it ſelfe.   Chap.8.page.102.
The Popiſh church is a church, though not a ſounde Church.
Chap.17.pag.147.148.149.151.andChap.23.pag.176.
*Whoſoeuer ſaycth or writeth that our Queene is a Schif-
matique for ſeparating herſelfe & her ſubiects from the
popiſh Church, (if the popiſh Church be a Church in any
regard) maketh a groſſe and Popiſh collection: and is at
the leaſt an vnduetifull ſubiect.   Chap.17.page 151.*
*Whether no more fellowſhip is to be had with papiſts in reli-
giō matters, then with pagane Idolaters.Cap.23.pa.181.*
*Amightie God neuer called any to the holy miniſtery either
in the old or new Teſtament, but he furniſhed them with
gifts fit for that holy function.   Chap.2.pag.55.56.&c.*
*Such as are in the miniſterie, and haue gifts in no meaſure,
ought to be remoued by the Magiſtrates and gouernours
of the Church.*   *Chap.9.page.110.*
*None vnbaptized may be a publique teacher in the viſible
Church.*   *Chap.8.page.93.*
*Popiſh prieſts haue a calling, though a faultie one.Chap.18.
page 154.155.*
*The approbation of the Church, maketh him a miniſter to
vs, which is not called by almighty God. Cap.12.pa.132.*
*They were ſacrifices and Sacraments, which were deliue-
red by the ignorant Leuiticall Prieſtes. Chap.8.pa.104.*
The godly are not polluted which receiue the Sacraments at

G.   the

A TABLE OF DIVERS

groſſe errours and Anabaptiſticall fan-
cies, conteined in _M. Penryes_
Treatiſe,&c.

After _Penry_ ſaith, That the life of the Magiſtracie is neither preſcribed in the worde(for ſo there could be no Magiſtrates out of the Church, nor any in the Church, but ſuch as are preſcribed in the word, which were impious to thinke) nor conteined in the gifts of the Magiſtracie, nor yet ſeparated from his outwarde calling: For the very outward calling, is it that giueth life vnto the Magiſtracie, though the perſon ſuſtei-ning it, want gifts to diſcharge the ſame. The reaſon hereof is euident, be-cauſe the Magiſtracie being an humaine conſtitution, as the holy Ghoſt ſaith 1. Pet.2.13. is appropriated vnto his poſſeſſion, ypõ whomſoeuer man beſtoweth the ſame, if hee be capable to poſſeſſe (though vnfit to execute) what is alotted vnto him. In his addition page 48.

This ſpeach of M. Penryes _is very groſſe. His firſt reaſon is this : there may be Magiſtrates out of the Church, therefore the life of the Magiſtracie is not preſcri-bed in the word._ M. P. _Antecedent is true: For Pharao, Nero, Iulian were magi-ſtrates out of the Church. I deny his argument : My reaſon is : the gifts of courage, fearing God, dealing truly, hating couetouſnes, which are the life of the Magiſtrate, are preſcribed in Gods booke,_ Exo.18.21. Deu.1.13. _If you ſay they are not the life of the magiſtracie, you diſſent from all the learned, and therfore muſt ſet downe what God requireth of him, that ſhould be his Magiſtrate._

His ſecond reaſon is this: There are and may be magiſtrates within the Church, which are not garniſhed with the aboue named gifts : therefore the life of the Ma-giſtracie is not preſcribed in the word. My anſwere is, I confeſſe that abſurd Ma-giſtrates haue bene and are many times aduanced in the Church, (I graunt they ſhould not) either by the corruption or errour of the electours: But I deny your ar-gument: My reaſon is: It is great wickednes to thinke, becauſe groſſe Electours pre-ferre vnfit men and ſo faile in their duetie, that Almightie God hath failed in pre-ſcribing what kinde of men he would haue to be his lieutenants.

M. Penry _addeth, that the life of the Magiſtracie is not conteined in the gifts of the magiſtracie. I diſſent from him in this. If he had ſaid, that the birth of the magi-ſtracie is not conteined in the gifts of the magiſtracie, he had hit the white._

M. Penry _writeth that the life of the magiſtracie is not ſeparated from his out-ward calling for the very outward calling, ſaith he, is it that giueth life vnto the magiſtracie. If this were true, then the life and birth of the magiſtrate are_ idem tempore, _that is, twinnes : and conſequently whoſoeuer hath the outwarde calling which is the birth, hath the inwarde calling which is the life of the magiſtrate. So is Gods furniture tyed to the electours voices, as to the chaire, and the inward & out-ward calling of the magiſtrate confounded, which is a palpable errour. If there bee an outward calling to the magiſtracie, without the which no man(howſoeuer furni-ſhed within)may preſume to execute the office of the magiſtrate, I am ſure there is an inward calling to the magiſtracie : For the outwarde calling doeth import an in-_

ward.

ward. If there be an inward calling which is by God himselfe, what I beseech you is it but such furniture and gifts, as are prescribed and required in the holy word?

The foundation whereupon M. Penry *hath built his former absurdities, is a very rotten post, that is, a grosse deprauing of a text of Scripture, viz.* The Magistracie is an humaine ordinance, 1.Pet.2.13. *that is, a deuise of man, and not an Ecclesiasticall constitution prescribed in the worde. That the magistracie is not any deuise of man, but Gods ordinance for the benefite of man, is a cleare trueth in Gods booke. None doubt of it, vnlesse they be Anabaptists or extremely ignorant.*

M. Penry faith that the word barely read and to no other purpofe then to edifie by reading, is not holfome doctrine. Chap.8.pag.99.

This is a blasphemous absurditie. M. Pentryes *reasons for it are most absurd and childish. I referre you to my answere. Chap.8.pag.* 100.101. *and to a proposition which I haue handled. Chap.4.pag.62. &c.*

M. Penry writeth that it is falfe to fay that the recitall of the fumme of Chriftes Sermon, that is, the word of inftitution, &c.is an edifying word: he faith it mainteyneth charming. Chap.8.pag.88.89.

This is a blasphemous absurditie. If euery part of the Canonical Scripture doth edifie, I trust the summe of the Lord Iesus Sermon ought to haue singuler allowance. If it ought to haue singuler allowance, it may not be indited and arraigned for maintenance of charming.

M. Penry faith that the people cannot fanctifie a Sabboth without a Sermon.His words are thefe: They are no minifters, whofe flocks by their miniftery can not fanctifie the Sabboth : our Readers are fuch, &c. In his addition. pag.60.

M. Penry accounteth the publique reading of the holy Scripture and publique prayers, no part of the sanctification of the Sabboth. If he had said that the Sabboth is not so well sanctified without, as with a godly Sermon, I woulde haue a-greed vnto him.

M. Penry maketh the perfon to giue credite to the holy word. His wordes are thefe: The word of God vttered, is not an edifying word, vnleffe it be vttered according to the ordinance, both in regard of the perfons that vtter the fame, and the ende wherefore it is vttered. Chap.8.pag.99.

This is a Popish errour : for the Scripture is ἀυτόπιστος, *that is, of credite in it selfe. Reade my answere. Chap.8.pag.102.*

M. Penry faith that there is no Church at all in Popery. Chap.23. pag. 175.176.

This is a grosse errour, condemned of very famous men and all reformed Churches. If there be no church at all in Popery, these absurdities will followe : first, the Pope is not Antichrist : Secondly, the infants of Papists may not be bapti-zed in any reformed Church, though some of the Religion doe present them to Baptisme, and publiquely vndertake the good education of them. Reade that which I haue written, Chap.17.pag.147.148.149.and Chap.23.pag.176.

M. Penry faith that if there be a Church in Popery, our Magiftrates, &c. are Schifmatiques, inafmuch as they haue feparated themfelues from the Church of Rome. Chap.17.pag.151.

This is a grosse and Papish collection, and cannot stand with the duetie of a sub-iect.

iect. *Reade my anſwere.Chap.17.pag.151.152.*

M. Penry writeth that men in the Popiſh Church are not ingraffed by Baptiſme into a true Chriſt. His wordes are theſe : Where there is no true Chriſt whereunto men can be ingraffed by Baptiſme, there true Baptiſme as touching the ſubſtance cannot be gotten,&c. But in Popery there is no true Chriſt whereinto men may be ingraffed,&c.   Chap.23.pag.173.

This is a groſſe errour condemned of all famous writers and Churches. Reade that which I haue written. Chap.23.pag.173.& 174.and cha.20.pag.156.157.

Maiſter *Penry* writeth that if baptiſme adminiſtred by vnpreaching mi- niſters, were denied to be a Sacrament, he would wiſh none to offer them- ſelues to that holy Sacrament for ſixe cauſes.

Firſt, we are already receyued into the boſome of the Church, and ac- knowledged to haue the ſeale of the couenant, in as much as we were once offered and receyued into the number of the godly by the outwarde ele- mēt,though corruptly. To what end then ſhould baptiſme ſerue vs againe ? In his exhort. to the gouernonrs,&c.of Wales.pag.31.

If this be true which M. Penry *ſaith, the outwarde and bare element deliuered by him,which in* M.Penryes *iudgement, is no miniſter,is the ſeale of Gods co- uenant: Which is a moſt abſurd hereſie.*

Secondly,the abſolute neceſſitie of baptiſme to ſaluation,by this meanes might ſeeme to be mainteined.

Falſe : They which require men vnbaptized, to offer themſelues to Baptiſme, are perſwaded that the contempt of the Sacrament is damnable : they doe not thinke that all which die without Baptiſme, (if contempt bee abſent) are dam- ned. Beſides,Baptiſme is neceſſarie in reſpect of our obedience : but, what obedi- ence is performed,when Baptiſme is refuſed?

Thirdly,leaſt wee ſhould ſeeme to agree with the heretical Catabaptiſts.

If no Baptiſme was deliuered by vnpreaching miniſters, M.Penry *is an here- ticall Catabaptiſt, if hee dehort any ſuch from holy Baptiſme, as were baptized by vnpreaching miniſters.*

Fourthly,other Churches haue not publikely decided the cauſe.

They needed not.They made no queſtion of it: for,with one voyce they condemne your Anabaptiſticall fancies.

Fiftly,that the practiſe ſhould not enforce them to bee rebaptized,which haue bene alreadie baptized,by ſuch as had commiſſion from the Lord to deale in thoſe myſteries.

If they be already baptized, no reaſon they ſhould deſire a ſecond Baptiſme: for Baptiſme may not be iterated. I haue prooued this point in my Treatiſe of the Sacraments,and in this booke. Chap.19.pag.156.

Laſtly,they, who (being nowe in the age of diſcretion) haue beene bapti- zed by Idoll miniſters,are either called or not called to ſaluation.If called, why ſhould they be rebaptized,ſeeing alreadie they haue bene made par- takers of the outward element, and accompted in the number of Chriſti- ans ? If not called,neither ſhould they be baptized,vntill they declared by their workes that they were Gods children.

If they receiued the Sacrament before, they neede not. If they receiued no Sa-

*crament,they cannot absteine from Baptisme,without intollerable,both sinne,and vengeance. None that are effectually called, either haue or will refuse to offer themselues to Baptisme: which Baptisme,before,they had not.Cornelius example,doeth teach vs that,*Acts.10. *Yea, I dare be bold to say,that her Maiesties subiects which are vnbaptized,and do not offer themselues to Baptisme, are not as yet effectually called,whatsoeuer either they or you pretend. The reason is, None are effectually called, which are not within the compasse of Gods couenant.The words of Gods couenant are these :* I will be thy God and the God of thy seede.Gen.17. *Are they within the compasse of this couenant,which either wittingly omit, or wilfully refuse Baptisme,which is the seale of Gods couenant?*

M. Penry sayth, that the preaching of the worde is necessarily required in the administration of Baptisme.chap.7 pag.82.

If this were true,al such as were Baptized without a Sermon,receiued no Sacrament. I referre you to my answere,Chap.7.pag.84.

M. Penry sayeth that Baptisme is not out of the Church. Chap.23.pag. 176.

This is a grosse errour.Reade that which I haue written.Chap.21.pag.158.&c.

M. Penryes iudgement is,that Queene Elizabeth and many thousandes in England are vnbaptized.

That his iudgement is such,I proue it by his owne wordes.He writeth thus,&c. In Popery there is no true Christ whereunto men may be ingraffed, &c. And a litle before : What Baptisme is that which is not an ingraffing into the true Christ? Chap.23.pag.173.A litle after he hath these words:There is no Church at all in Popery. chap.23.pag.175.176. And in an other place,&c. that Baptisme is not out of the Church. If M. Penry shall answere that it was Baptisme in the Popish church yesterday,but it is not so either to day or to morowe, because the Christ professed now in Popery is not a true but a deuided Christ, I must needes tell him that Christ in the Popish profession was diuided as well when her Maiestie,&c. was Baptized,as he is deuided in the Popish profession at this day. Besides M. Penry writeth that the Popish church was neuer the Temple of God since Antichrist planted his pestilent chaire therein. Chap.22. pag.165. To conclude, seeing there is in M.Penryes iudgement no Church,no Baptisme,no Ministery in the Popish church,&c.I may be bold to affirme that in M. Penryes iudgement her Maiestie and many thousandes more are vnbaptized.

M.Penry saith that the holy Supper is an extraordinary Sacrament which is deliuered priuately by a Minister. Chap.14.pag.139.

This error is condemned by M.Caluine,*whose resolution is, that it is lawfull to administer the holy Supper priuately, if certaine cautions be obserued. I rest in his iudgement. I referre you to chap.15,page 141.142.*

M.Penry saith that they which comunicate with vnpreaching ministers, approue the sinne of the vnpreaching ministerie. Chap.10.pag.119.

This is an Anabaptisticall fancie: for S.Paul (*as* M.Penry *writeth*) *communicated after his conuersion with those priestes which were as vnlearned as euer any.chap.11.pag.128.I referre you besides to my answere. chap.10.pag.119.*

M.Penry

M. Penry is bolde to control Almightie God, for barring the vncircumcifed Ifraelites from eating the Pafchall lambe : His words are thefe, why
fhould the godly of the family be excluded from the action, the caufe why
they were vncircumcifed not being in them? Chap.8.pag.89.

This is intollerable faucinefſe: It becommeth not duſt and aſhes to diſpute with,
and to coūtermand the Maieſtie of God. Reade my anſwere, chap.8.pag.91.92.

M. Penries iudgement is, that the touching of a dead man, which was a
legall vncleannes, was finne, Chap.9.page.110.

For proofe of this errour, he quoteth two textes of Scripture moſt abſurdly. I
referre you to my anſwere. chap.9.page.111.112.113.

M. Penry faith, that Caiphas high prieſthood was the Lords ordinance.
Chap.10.page 122.

This is an errour : for the Lords ordināce was, that only one ſhould be the high
prieſt: and it is manifeſt in the text, that Annas & Caiphas were high prieſts
together, luke 3.

M. Penry fayth, that he is aſſured that popiſh prieſts are no miniſters,
that is, that they haue no calling at all. Chap.22.page 160.162.163.

If this were true, firſt, a great number are vnbaptized. Secondly, Caluine, Be-
za, and other famous men and churches (which I do not thinke) do erre groſly.
Laſtly, only M. Penries iudgement is found, which (I am ſure) is a moſt abſurd
iudgement. Reade my anſwere, cap.22.pag.161.162.163. and cap.18.pag.154.

M. Penry affirmeth readers to be no miniſters, and for any thing that is
reuealed in the worde, that they can deliuer no Sacrament, and yet that
which hath bene done by them, may be a Sacrament : and what contra-
rietie (faith hee) is there in thefe aſſertions? In his exhort. to the Gouernours &c. of Wales, pag.32.

Then yeſterday a Sacrament, and to morowe none. Goodly diuinitie. Such Saint,
ſuch ſhrine.

M. Penry fayth, that he hath no miniſterie, which finneth in executing
the workes of the miniſterie, as adminiſtring Sacraments &c. His wordes
are thefe : the calling of an vnpreaching miniſter, is not the calling of the
miniſterie, becaufe he finneth in intermedling with the workes thereof.
Chap.25.

If this were true, the contentious miniſters of Philippi, were no miniſters: for,
they ſinned in executing the workes of the miniſterie. That appeareth in thefe
wordes of the Apoſtle: Some preach Chriſt through enuie and ſtrife, Phi.1.15.
Beſides, M. Penries ignorant Leuites were no prieſts in the old Teſtament: for
they ſinned in executing the prieſthood.

That the outward approbation of the Church, doth not make a miniſter.
Chap.12.page 131.

If he meane, that it doth not furniſh a miniſter with knowledge, I graunt it. If
he meane that it doth not make him a miniſter to vs, then were the ignorant
Leuiticall prieſts no prieſts in the Iewiſh Church. Which ignorant Leuiticall
prieſts, in M. Penries iudgement, were lawfull prieſts, though not good prieſts.
Chap.11.page 125. reade my anſwere, chap.12.page 132.

M. Penry fayth, that vnfitneſſe to teach, made not a nullitie of the Leuiticall

ticall priefts office. Chap.11.page 125.

M. Penry fayth in an other place , that no minifterie is feperated from a gift.
Againe,whofoeuer preferueth not knowledge in his lippes, is no minifter: in his
addition page 57.58. Againe,to make a minifter,there be two things required:
Firft, a being or life, which the Lord onely can giue : Secondly, a birth, which
the Church,as an inftrument of the ordinance of God,is to beftowe vpon him by
his outward calling.Thefe two things are fo effentially to be required in a mini-
fter , that whofoeuer wanteth either of them , he cannot poffibly be a minifter.
Againe,be it,that a man haue the outward calling of the Church: yet in deede,
he is no minifter, vnleffe the Lorde hath giuen him the life of a minifter , by
committing the word of reconciliation vnto his hands: in his addi.page 45.46.
M.Penry erreth greatly eyther in his firft,or laft propofitions.If he can recon-
cile them, hee can worke miracles. The tougheft glewe that is, can not make
them cleaue together.

M. Penry offers difputation. Chap.16.page 143.

Infcitia audax : none fo bold as blind bayard.Reade my anfwere. Chap.16.page
143.144.

M. Penry hath thefe wordes : I dare arreft and attaint of high treafon a-
gainft the maieftie of the Higheft , all both men and Angels , who eyther
defend the communicating with vnpreaching minifters, lawfull, or communicate with them: in his addition page 65.

Sefquipedalia verba : euery worde as bigge as a houfe : Great fmoke , but no
fire, thankes be to God. Your arreft is like Goliaths curfe : it is not fo fearefull
as paper fhot.

Thus M. Penry hath troubled HEAVEN, CHVRCH,
COMMON-VVEALTH, and HIMSELFE. HEAVEN,for
he being duft and afhes, hath beene too bolde and fawcie
with God himfelfe: CHVRCH, for he hath offered vnto
it for treafure , not coales, which had bene very bafe, but
poifon,which is very dangerous: COMMON-VVEALTH,
for he hath vndermined the chaire of the Magiftrat:I hope
fuch conies will be looked vnto: HIMSELFE, for he hath
contriued and broched many proud,blafphemous,& Anabaptifticall fancies. I perceiue it is true which that famous
man M. *Caluine* hath written,viz. that an Anabaptifticall
head is *immenfum deliriorum mare* ,a vaft Sea of dotages.
Calu. contra Anabapt.

A DE-

A DEFENCE OF SVCH

points in R.S o m e s laſt treatiſe, as M.Penry hath
dealt againſt.

R. Some.

Before that I anſwere *M.Penryes* booke, I am to
deſire the godly Reader to conſider weightily of this
litle which followeth.   My two firſt propoſitions
which *M. Penry* dealeth againſt,are.

1. *They which were baptized inthe Popiſh Church
   by Popiſh Prieſtes, receiued true Baptiſme,
   touching the ſubſtance of Baptiſme.*

2. *They are the Sacraments of Baptiſme and the
   holy Supper,which are deliuered in the Church
   of England by vnpreaching miniſters.*

I. Penry.

Ou handle two needeleſſe pointes. Firſt,that
They which were baptized by Popiſh Prieſts &c.
Secondly,that *They are the Sacraments of Baptiſme, &c.* In theſe two pointes *M.Some*,you
haue proued nothing that my writings haue
denied.

R. Some.

I doe ſee as yet no difference
betwene vs. If *M.Penry* denieth
them not to be Sacraments which are adminiſtred
by Popiſh prieſts & vnpreaching Miniſters,hee can
not deny Popiſh prieſts and vnpreaching Miniſters
to haue a calling,&c. For it is a rule in D iuinitie:*Sa-*
cramentum

H.

cramentum nullum sine ministro, that is, No Sacrament without a minister. My thirde propofition which *M. Penry* cenfureth, is.

3 *The godly are not polluted which receiue the Sacrament at the handes of an unpreaching Minister.*

I. Penry.

Paul communicated fince his conuerfion with thofe Priefts that were as vnlearned as euer any. Which he would not haue done if inabilitie to teach had made them no Prieftes.

R. Some.

Then in *M. Penryes* iudgement, the holy Apoftle was not polluted by communicating with vnpreaching Minifters. Can any man (if he haue but halfe an eye) fufpect that *M. Penry* diffenteth from me in iudgement? What then may I thinke, againft whom he hath written? Well, I muft be content with the meafure he offereth me. My comfort is, that he fhall gaine, and I lofe nothing by it. Yea, I affure my felfe by Gods grace that Gods Church fhal gaine by this difference. Hee pretendeth great defire of a learned Minifterie: but his eagre defence of ignorāt Leuiticall priefts, bewrayeth him. If I had written fo much for ignorant Minifters, the great bell had bene rung out before this. I fhould haue had it on both fides of mine eares. I haue dealt very earneftly and humbly by writings and fpeache for a learned Minifterie. I haue receiued very comfortable anfwere of very great and honourable perfonages : who haue alreadie (thankes be to God) employed fome, and will, I doubt not, employ more in the Churches feruice. The Lord increafe that bleffing for his Chrifts fake.

The

The marke,I feare,which *M.Penry* leauels at,is,simply to condemne the outwarde calling of the Ministers in our Church : and so to shake hands with the Anabaptisticall Recusants. Though he hit not that white, hee will hardly misse that Butte. If hee bee throughly searched , it is not vnlike to fall out so. Some part of his writings looke shrewdly that way.

CHAP. 2.

ALMIGHTIE GOD NEVER

called any to the holy ministerie,either in the olde or newe Testament, but he furnished them with giftes fitte for that holy function.

HE Israelites liued in slauerie and drudgerie in Egypt. They were as rude & grosse as might be. When the Lord would make his Tabernacle, he furnished *Bezaleel* & *Aholiab* of the tribes of *Iuda* & *Dan*,for that excellent worke. He gaue them skill in working all kind of broiderie,*Exo.31.*& *36.chap*.When *Salomons* Temple should be built , Almightie God furnished *Hiram* of *Tyrus* for that stately worke, *1.Kin.7*. If Almightie God , for the framing and building of the Tabernacle and Temple, which were figures of the Church, did so excellently beautifie *Bezaleel, Aholiab* and *Hiram* : it is great wickednesse to thinke, that his Maiestie did euer send any vnfurnished to build his spirituall Tabernacle and Temple, which is his spouse,bodie,Citie,&c.

When the Lord commaunded *Aaron, Eleazar,*

&c. to be confecrated his Priefts, and confequently to teach, to pray for the Ifraelites, and to offer facrifices, (in which three branches, the Priefts office confifted) he furnifhed them with excellent furniture for that honourable feruice. The words of God himfelfe are cleare for this: *My couenant was with Leui of life and peace, and I gaue him feare, and he feared me, and was afraide before my Name. The Lawe of trueth was in his mouth, and there was no iniquitie found in his lips: he walked with me in peace and equitie, and did turne many away from iniquitie. Mal. 2.*

It is a pofitiue law of Almightie God: *The Priefts lips fhall keepe knowledge, &c. Mal. 2.* It is a Canon of the Apoftle: *A minifter muft be apt to teach, 1. Tim. 3.* If Almightie God had by any warrant of his, commended the Ifraelites heretofore to the charge of ignorant Leuites, or his Church fince to ignorant minifters, he had broken a ftatute lawe and Canon of his owne, and had bin greatly touched in honor.

Thofe Leuiticall priefts were fent of God, and paftors according to his heart, which were able to feede Gods people with knowledge and vnderftanding, *Iere. 3.*

Thofe Leuitical priefts which were vnfit to teach, were neuer of Gods fending, though they were of the line of *Aaron.* Almightie God difclaimes them in thefe wordes: *My people are deftroyed for lacke of knowledge: becaufe thou haft refufed knowledge, I will alfo refufe thee, that thou fhalt be no prieft to me, Hofe. 4.*

Efay was a famous man for birth and eloquence. Before that hee was fent to denounce and deliuer Gods iudgements and mercies to *Ierufalem* and *Iuda &c,* the Lorde did fingularly furnifh him with knowledge,

knowledge,ſpeach, courage &c. *Eſa.6.* and *50.Chap.*
Ieremy was an excellent Prophet. When the Lord
would vſe his ſeruice, he touched his mouth, furniſhed his heart,&c. *Iere.1.* In like ſort dealt Almightie God with *Micheas:* he made him a complete man,
Mich.3.

    Elizeus attended on the plough, *1.Kin.19. Amos*
on the herde, *Amos 1.* and *7.Chap.* The Lorde did not
vſe the miniſterie of *Elizeus* and *Amos,* vntil he had
furniſhed them with skill, wiſedome, courage, &c.

    Our Sauiour Chriſt did not ſend any vniuerſitie
men at the firſt to preach the Goſpel, leaſt the conuerſion of men ſhould be attributed to learning and
eloquence. He called rude and baſe men from their
occupatiōs to be his Apoſtles. Before he ſent them
to be his trumpets, & to deliuer his meſſage, he caſt
them (as it were) into a newe molde, he gaue them
ſpeciall furniture, *Iohn 20. Act.2.* If the Lorde Ieſus
had not dealt thus with them, how could they haue
acquited themſelues in preaching and diſputation
as they did? for they attended before, on fiſhing and
other trades.

    Saint Paul ſetting out in orient colours, the lar-
geſſe and bountie of our Sauiour Chriſt to his
Church after his Aſcenſion, hath theſe wordes : *He
gaue ſome to bee Apoſtles, and ſome Prophets, and ſome E-
uangeliſts, and ſome Paſtors and Teachers, for the gathering together of the Saints, for the worke of the miniſterie,
and for the edification of the body of Chriſt, Eph.4.* If theſe
here mentioned had bin vnfurniſhed : Firſt, Chriſts
gift had beene no benefite, but a burthen. Secondly, how ſhoulde the Saints haue bene gathered, his
body built, his ſheepe fed, his ſpouſe garniſhed?

       H.iij.   Thoſe

Thofe Princes and Captaines which fend vnskilfull Ambaffadours & vntrained fouldiers on ambaf-
fade and warfare,doe greatly ftayne and difhonour
themfelues. Almightie God, which is the greateft
Prince and moft valiant Captaine, did neuer fault
in this. If he had, hee had giuen his glory and the
Church a grieuous blowe. I confeffe, God giues
not to all his feruants, like furniture. Some haue
ten,fome,fiue: fome,two: fome,one talent, which
talēts muft neither be buried in the earth,nor wrap-
ped in a napkin. If they be vfed,they will multiplie
as the loaues in the Gofpel. They which cannot
feede with manchet, muft feede with barlie bread.
Rammes fkinnes & goates haire were amongft the
holy offrings, as well as gold, filuer, braffe, pur-
ple,&c.*Exod.25.*

If none are called by almightie God to the holy
minifterie,but fuch as he hath furnifhed with giftes
in fome meafure: it is the duety of the ciuill and ecclefiafticall magiftrates to prouide, that ignorant
men which are not acquainted with Gods booke,
be kept and thruft out of the holy minifterie, vnlefle
they will be partakers of great finnes, and confequently of great plagues. A fufficient teacher is a
rare bleffing: for he fetteth the Lords plough for-
ward, and is Gods hand to deliuer heauenly trea-
fures. If good care fhall be had by our Prince, our
Bifhops, our Patrons, to goe on in aduancing and
making choife of fuch both gouernors and paftors:
Gods religion, Church, Vniuerfities, will flourifh
more notably, and confequently Gods glory: our
gracious Prince fhall be more foundly honoured:
the people of the land fhall be fingularly encoura-
ged.

ged to ferue God, to fight for the religion, for their
Prince, for their countrey, againft any, either for-
raine or home enemie : and Gods fauour and bleffings fhall be multiplied vpon our Queene, vpon vs,
and vpon our pofteritie. Almightie God will accept this at our hands for great thankfulnes for his
late mercy in preferuing the Englifh both fleet and
nation, and amazing & difperfing the popifh fleet,
by his mighty hand . This gracious and notable fauour of God hath danted Gods & our enemies in al
popifh kingdomes and churches : and hath put life
into Gods feruants, in all nations & Churches that
profeffe the religion. The Lord for his Chriftes fake
graunt, that we may be reuerently mindfull of, and
humbly thankfull to his maieftie for this deliue-
rance. And, that as in the time of danger, we vfed the
83. and 68. pfalmes, to entreate Gods fauour : fo we
may euer fing the 124. and 46. pfalmes., to publifh
Gods mercie, and to teftifie our thankfulnes for this
gracious conqueft.

Chap. 3.

ALMIGHTIE GOD NEVER
called any to Magiftracie, but hee furnifhed them accordingly.

He Egyptians were harde mafters to
the Ifraelites. They kept them very
fhort in Egypt. When almighty God
would bleffe the Ifraelites w̄ freedom
and gouernment, he furnifhed *Mofes*
notably for that excellent feruice. He gaue him finguler

guler wifedome, courage,&c. If he had not, *Mofes* had bene vtterly vnfit for fuch a famous match.

Mofes complained vnto the Lorde, that hee alone was not able to gouerne the Ifraelites. Almightie God, for the eafe of *Mofes* appointed 70, Elders of Ifrael to help in that gouernment. That thofe Ancients might cary thefelues profitably in that charge, the Lord did garnifh them accordingly. *Num.11.*

Mofes before his death, defired the Lorde to appoint one to fucceede him in the gouernment, that the Ifraelites might not be as fheepe without a fhepheard, *Num.27.* Gods pleafure was that *Iofua* fhould be the man, *Deut.34.* He did fo affift and furnifh him with the feare of God, with the fpirit of wifedome, courage , &c. that he became very famous , in peace, in warre, at, and after his dying day.

The Church & common wealth of the Ifraelites, decayed greatly, & were at a low ebbe in king *Sauls* time. That both Church and cōmon wealth might be reuiued, the Lord aduanced his feruant *Dauid* to the kingdome. He did beautifie him with extraordinary graces, as with precious Diamonds. *Dauid* was very religious, very wife, very valiant : very religious, for hee brought home the Lordes Arke : very wife, for his royal throne was a feate of Iuftice : very valiant, for he vanquifhed many enemies.

Salomō fucceeded his father *Dauid* in the gouernment of the Ifraelites. That he might cary himfelfe accordingly in that great charge, he defired and obtained at Gods hands, *a wife and vnderftanding heart.* *1.King 3.*

Shebna was a great officer in *Ezechias* Court. His courfe was cunning and dangerous to the common
wealth

wealth of *Iuda*. Almightie God coulde not beare
him, therefore sent a notable vengeance vpon him.
In his steade, *Eliakim* was appointed vnder the King
of *Iuda*: A man singularly furnished by the Lord, for
he was a father of the inhabitants of *Ierusalem*, and
of the house of *Iuda*. *Esay 22*.

Ioseph was aduanced in *Egypt*: *Nehemias* in *Persia*:
Daniel in *Chaldea*. They dealt excellently in their
gouernment: for, almightie God did notable fur-
nish them.

Gedeon was a very meane man: he attended on the
flaile. In his time the Madianites were heauie to the
Israelites 7. yeeres. That the Lord might deliuer his
people from the tyrannie of the Madianites, he furnished *Gedeon* for that seruice in extraordinary sort.
Iudg. 6 and 7. chap. There were in *Gedeon* which ought
to be in euery Captaine both by sea and land, *Scien-
tia rei militaris, virtus, authoritas, felicitas. Cic. pro lege
Manil*. That is, skil in warlike affaires, vertue, authoritie, felicitie.

They which are inwardly called to the Magistracie, are such as are furnished by the Lord with good
parts for that weighty function. They are not brambles, as *Abimelech* was, nor sots, as *Maximinus* was,
nor fooles, as *Candaules* was. They are vine, figge,
oliue trees, as *Dauid, Ezechias, Iosaphat, Constantinus*
were. These are such Magistrates in whom God de-
lighteth, and which are best welcome to Gods people: for, they are rare ornaments both of Church
and common wealth. God increase the number of
such in this lande, that both Church and common
wealth, may shine continually as starres at home,
abroade, &c. to the glory of God, the honour of the

Prince, the terrour of the enemie, and the comfort of the Englifh nation.

CHAP. 4.

THE READING OF THE
holy Scripture doth edifie.

Ofes commaunded the Priefts in this fort, &c. *VVhen all Ifrael fhall come to appeare before the Lord thy God, in the place which he fhall chufe, thou fhalt reade this lawe before all Ifrael , that they may heare it. Gather the people together: men and women, and children, and thy ftranger that is within thy gates, that they may heare, and that they may learne, and feare the Lord your God, and keepe, and obferue all the wordes of this law. And that their children which haue not knowen it, may heare it, and learne to feare the Lord your God, &c. Deut. 31.* I gather my argument out of this place thus. By reading of the lawe of God , the Ifraelites did learne and feare God : therefore they were edified. If you reply that all the Ifraelites did not profite by this reading, I anfwere, no more did all profit by the preaching of the Prophets, of *Chrift* and the Apoftles. The fault was not in the feed, but in the ground. Vnleffe Gods fpirit touch our hearts, as the worde doeth pearce our eares, Gods truth either read or preached is a fhut booke, and as a fealed letter vnto vs.

When hee fhall fit vpon the throne of his kingdome, then fhall he write him this lawe repeated in a booke, by the Priefts of the Leuites. And it fhall be with him, and he fhall

                                        reade

reade therein all dayes of his life, that hee may learne to
feare the Lorde his God,and to keepe all the woordes of this
lawe,and thefe ordinances,for to doe them : That his heart
be not lifted vp aboue his brethren, and that hee turne not
from the commandement, to the right hand or to the left,
but that he may prolong his dayes in his kingdome, hee,and
his fonnes in the middes of Ifrael. Deut.17. I frame my
argument thus. The king is commaunded to reade
the lawe of God, that hee may learne to feare God,
and decline pride: therefore the reading of the law
of God doth edifie.

In king *Iofias* time, the booke of the lawe was
found by *Hilkiah* the Prieft. This booke was read in
the Lordes houfe.The king was prefent: fo were all
the men of *Iuda*, &the inhabitants of *Ierufalem*, and
the Priefts,and the Leuites,and all the people from
the greateft to the fmalleft, &c. *2.Chron.34.* I make
my argument thus. The booke of the lawe was not
read in vaine in the Lordes houfe, &c.*2.Kings 22.*
therefore it did edifie.

All the wordes of my mouth are righteous , there
is no lewdnefſe, nor frowardneſſe in them. They are all
plaine to him that will vnderftande, and ftreight to them
that would find knowledge.Prou.8. Therefore the holy
Scriptures both read and preached,doe edifie. *His*
falubriter, praua corriguntur,parua nutriuntur , magna
oblectantur ingenia.Aug. Epift.3. The holy Scripture
hath in it, milke for babes , and ftronger meate for
them that are of age.*Heb.5.* The holy Scripture ,is
a fhallowe water,wherein the lambe may wade,and
a great fea,wherein the Elephant may fwimme.

The Lawe and the Prophets were read in the
Churches of *Antiochia*,and *Ierufalem. Act.13.* and in

Nazareth.

Nazareth.Luke 4. If the reading of the holy Scriptures doe not edifie, why were the law and Prophets read in the Temple and Synagogues?

The Apoſtle writeth thus to the paſtours and people of *Coloſſe* : *Let the worde of Chriſt dwell in you plenteouſly, &c. Coloſſ. 3.* Therefore Gods people are not to be barred from the reading of the holy Scripture. If it doeth not edifie, they were iuſtly barred by the Popiſh Cleargie.

Victorinus was an Oratour in *Rome.* By reading the Scriptures he became a Chriſtian : *Mirante Roma, gaudente ecclesia :* that is, *Rome* marueyled at *Victorinus* conuerſion : Gods Church was glad of it, *Aug. Confeſſ. lib. 8. cap. 2.*

Gods ſpeach vnto vs, I am ſure, doth edifie: when the Scriptures are read, God ſpeaketh vnto vs. The holy Scriptures are *Dei Epiſtola. &c.* that is, Gods Epiſtle vnto vs.

By reading the Scriptures, Gods people do more eaſily receiue Gods holy truth, and eſpie Popiſh abſurdities and Anabaptiſticall fancies.

They which miſlike the reading of the ſcriptures, are *Zwingfildians,* that is, abſurde heretikes. What then is maſter *Penry,* which writeth that the worde barely read, and to no other purpoſe then to edifie by reading, is not wholeſome doctrine?

If any ſhall gather of this I haue ſet downe, that I am an enemie to the preaching of the word, hee deſerueth no anſwere. My iudgement is: If the reading of the holy ſcriptures doeth edifie, that ſounde preaching doeth edifie much more. By ſound preaching, I vnderſtand the giuing of the true ſenſe of the ſcripture, and applying it to the profite of the auditours.

auditours. Thus did *Ezra*, *Chrift*, the Apoſtles, preach. This courſe,I am ſure,doeth highly pleaſe God, and bringeth many ſheepe into the Lordes folde, The Lorde increaſe the number of ſuch tea-chers,that Gods religion may flouriſh as *Aarons* rod did , and that Popiſh and Anabaptiſticall errours may be deuoured as the roddes of the Egyptian ſor-cerers were.

Ille huic doctrinæ inimicus eſt animus, qui vel errando eam neſcit eſſe ſaluberrimam, vel odit ægrotando medicinam. Aguſt.Epiſt.3.

CHAP. 5.

A DEFENCE OF THAT
which hath bene written in the
queſtions of the ignorant miniſte-
rie and the communicating
with them:

By IOHN PENRY.

Here be two things (M. D. S o m e) wherein you by oppugning that trueth, which out of the worde of God I had ſet downe, concerning the two former queſtions,haue bene wanting both vnto your ſelfe and to the cauſe : the defence whereof you vnder-tooke. The former want of the two, appeareth by your ſpare dealing in a matter of ſuch great weight: wherin you haue dealt with ſo illiberal a hand,that what hath bene writ-ten by you, might ſeeme to proceede rather from any then from a man whoſe gifts and learning ſeemed to promiſe the affording of greater and more weightie matters, then any ſet downe in that treatiſe.

R.Some.

Your beginning is full of courage. I do not won-der at it.He that runneth alone, is alwayes formoſt. You accuſe me to withſtande Gods trueth. A ſore charge. If true,I muſt reuerſe my iudgement: if vn-true,

true,you haue dealt iniurioufly with me. When *Ioas*
was aduanced to the Imperiall Crowne of *Iuda*, *A-*
thalia cried, *Treafon*, *Treafon*. *2.Chron.23.*   A hard
fpeach againft king *Ioas,Iehoiada,&c.*But *Athalia* her
felfe was the Traitour. You fhall apply this. I haue
dealt, you fay, verie fparingly in a matter of great
importance. If I haue fo,your aduantage is greater.
If the feede fowen in my booke, were like yours, I
might be iuftly thought to bee verie prodigall. My
treatife,I perceiue,is not for your tooth: it is fimple
in your eye. *Aquila non capit mufcas.* It hath pleafed
many,I thanke God,of excellent learning and wifedome to like of it: That is my comfort. *Inftar mille*,
Platonis calculus. I make very meane account,as yet,
of your iudgement. You are not read, you are to
feeke in the principles of diuinitie, you haue broched groffe errours,you know not your ignorance.
For that knowledge which Almightie God hath giuen me, I thanke his Maieftie verie humbly. It is
more,I confeffe,then I am worthie of.God giue me
grace to vfe it to his glorie.

I. Penry.

   The number of my reafons were many:you onely haue touched two of
them,the reft are not dealt with. And therefore the caufe as yet remaineth whole. For, be it you had anfwered thefe two as you haue not, yet
had you not fatisfied the doubtfull confcience of thofe, that know not in
thefe points which way to turne them, as long as any one of my reafons
remayned vnanfwered.

R.Some,

   Your reafons, I confeffe, haue number: but they
want weight. I haue confuted three of them. The
firft of the three, is accompted by you a pillar of
marble. But I haue not, you fay,dealt with the reft.
Content your felfe:I haue made no fault.I anfwered
                                                      fuch

such and so many, as were deliuered to me by some
of your faction. When I had finished my treatise,
your booke was brought me: before, I knew not that
you were the father of them. You denie that I haue
answered any of your reasons. It is easie to say so,
and you might worst haue sayde it. A partie is vnfit
to be a Iudge. Your reasons are all of one stampe:
therefore the ouerthrow of the principall, is the o-
uerthrow of all. Your followers vvhich knowe not
which way to turne them, may thanke both you
and themselues: you, for sowing: themselues, for
reaping such giddie fancies, It is an easie thing to
leade and fall into an Anabaptisticall maze. They
will not bee satisfied, you say, before euery one of
your reasons bee answered. A peremptorie resolution. They are pinned belike on your sleeue. I hope
wee shall not haue a *Pythagoras* of you, Woulde you
haue your boisterous speech go for an Oracle, and
cary all as a violent streame before it? God forbid.
It were a hard case. I trust you desire it not. If you
doe, you are not like to haue it.

I.Penry.

In this point there is also another want, which I would had beene re-
dressed. And that is of two sortes. First, a manifest going from the controuersie: for the question being, whether ignorant men, not ordeyned of
God for the gathering together of the Saintes, bee ministers or no: you
leaue that, and proue the Sacraments administred by them, viz: by popish
priests, & our dumbe ministers, in the dayes of blindnes and ignorance, to
be sacraments, which is no part of the matter in controuersie, but an o-
ther point to be discussed (if men will be gotten at all to enter thereunto)
when the former is determined and decided.

R, Some.

Your speeches are very idle. I swarue not one iot
from the cause I dealt in. For proofe of this, consi-
der what I write. Certaine in *London* gaue out in my
hearing:

hearing: firft,that fuch as were baptized by Popifh Priefts in the Popifh Church, and by vnpreaching minifters in our Church,receiued no baptifme : Secondly,that the Godly were polluted, which receyued any Sacrament at the hands of vnpreaching minifters. To heale thefe fores, I was defired to prouide a plaifter. I did fo, and God hath giuen a good blefling vnto it. All this time your booke was as great a ftranger to me, as it is nowe to the Duke of *Medina.* What fay you M. *Penry* ? Haue I faulted as you imagine? Had you any the leaft caufe fo roughly to feaze vpon me, and to charge me with going from the point ? Bee iudge your felfe : yea, I refufe not the iudgement of your difciples, if they haue any dramme of equitie in them.

I. *Penry.*

Secondly, your reafons are fo fewe, and fo commonly knowen vnto al, that for their nun ber a fmall deale of paper might conteyne an anfwere vnto them : for their noueltie,they could not put a man that had according vnto knowledge,but once allowed of the caufe,to any great labour in anfwering them. As being things fo commonly obiected by al,learned or vnlearned,that hold our readers to be minifters,and thinke it lawfull to communicate with them, as by courfe of fpeech they fall vnto that difcourfe, where all men may eafily fee,that there was a great ouerfight committed by M *Some,* in deeming that the oppugning of a caufe countenanced by moft of the Godly learned,would bee taken in hand by any, who could not anfwere the reafons which he might be fure would be obiected by all.And who could bee ignorant, that the odious controuerfie, concerning the profanation of baptifme, both by Popifh Prieftes, and our dumbe Minifters, would offer it felfe in the forefront to withftande the trueth ? that the ciuill Magiftracie, the minifterie of the dumbe Leuites,the corrupt outwarde calling of our readers woulde require an anfwere,which are the reafons,and the onely reafons vfed by you.

R. *Some.*

If my arguments be fewe, I haue done you pleafure:for they are fooner anfwered. They haue, you fay,no noueltie : I like them the better: for they are

as

as I defired. If they bee not for your diet, I doe not paffe : my thought is taken. If nothing were good or bad, but that which you like or miflike, precious pearles fhould go for tile fherdes, and pebble ftones for Diamonds. *Tichonius* a Donatift faid of himfelfe and his fellowes: *Quod volumus, fanctum eft.* Your muficke, I hope, is not like his. If it bee, you are too imperiall: You will not be abidden. What, and how weake my reafons are, muft bee decided hereafter: for, your wordes are no arguments. If my reafons were futable to your anfweres, they were very wofull. Your odious fpeech that I withftand the trueth, is vfed often: it is a fpeciall flowre in your booke. This courfe hurts you and not me. It hurts you: for it bewrayes your humour. It hurts not me: for your tongue cannot difgrace me,

I.Penry.

The laft want I finde in you, is conteyned in the infufficiencie of your reafons, which euidently fhewe the infufficiencie of the conclufion, that would be inferred by them. Your reafons are all of them faultie, either becaufe they defire that for graunted which is the queftion, or make thofe things of like nature, wherein there is a great diffimilitude. From the firft of the two faults it commeth to paffe, that you take for graunted, that the writings of reuerend and godly men, as of *Auguftine,* M.*Beza,* &c. will proue that which the worde of the eternall God doth not warrant. Hence you take it granted, that Popifh Priefts were minifters : that the outward approbation of the Church, maketh a Minifter: that, whenfoeuer the word of inftitution is pronounced with the outwarde element, there muft prefently be a Sacrament: that, I take an euill Minifter for no Minifter: that, there was a nullitie both of *Caiphas* minifterie, becaufe he came in by briberie, and of the litigious Minifters in the Church of *Philippi,* &c. Howfoeuer you take thofe things as graunted principles, yet they are the poynts in controuerfie, and fo farre from being yeelded vnto by me, that I haue fhewed euery one of them to be manifeftly falfe.

R.Some.

You finde many faults. You are a hard man : you couer none. Moates with you are beames, and molhils

hils mountaines:yea,no moates and no molhils are beames and mountaines, if they appeare at your barre.It pleaſeth you to giue out that all my reaſons are faultie. If you meane in your eye, I doe eaſily graūt it: If you meane in the eye of the learned,you miſtake the matter. But what are the faultes which you purſue ſo hotly? Forſooth,I take that, you ſay, for graunted,which is the queſtion: viz.that Popiſh prieſts were miniſters: that whenſoeuer the word of inſtitution is added to the element,there is a Sacrament: and that ſuch a thing is thus and ſo, becauſe *Auguſtine* and *Beza* write ſo. Your tongue is no ſlander. Did I euer ſay or write that Popiſh prieſtes had a lawfull calling?I haue written(I confeſſe)that Popiſh prieſts haue a calling, though a faultie one. Of this iudgemēt are *Beza, Caluin,* the reformed Churches: But all theſe are wide of the Butte: onely you do hit the white:you wil teach them.*Sus Mineruam.* It becōmeth not the houſe. Did I euer ſay or write, that whenſoeuer the worde of Inſtitution is added to the elemēt, there muſt preſently be a Sacrament? There is no ſillable in my treatiſe, that lookes that way. You imagine I ſay ſo : and of this abſurd conceite,you conclude that priuate men,children,women,idiots (in my iudgemēt) may adminiſter a Sacramēt.You pretend great ſinceritie: but your dealing with me in this and ſome other points , is neither honeſt nor ſcholerlike. It ſhall appeare ſo by Gods grace in this booke.Theſe particulars,& that of *Caiphas* prieſthood, and of the contentious miniſters of *Philippi* , ſhall be handled in their ſeuerall places.

I.Penry.

I. Penry.

The diffimilitude is in the reafons drawen from the Leuiticall prieft-hood, and the ciuill magiftracie: with whom if you compare the minifterie of the new couenant, you fhall finde, firft, that you bring in a fimilitude to fhewe that which is not proued: and fecondl , that you make thofe to be twinnes, which all men muft needes graunt to be as vnlike, as crooked and ftraight lines are vnmatchable.

R. Some.

My fecond fault is, as you fay, in drawing an Argument from the Leuiticall priefthood to the miniſterie of the newe Teftament. Is this a fault? no, no: the fault is in your eye, not in my pen: but, why may I not drawe an argument, as I did from the Leuitical priefthood, to the minifterie of the new Teftament? Your reafon is : the Leuiticall priefthood and the minifterie of the new Teftament are not twins, are vnmatchable, they cānot ftand together : therefore a reafon cannot be drawen from the one to the other. You take this, I am fure, to be an inuincible argument: but it is as ftrong as a rope of fand. I denie your argument. My reafons are: firft, *Aaron* did not take the priefthood vpõ him before he was called: therefore none in our time, may enter into the minifterie, vnleffe he be called. This argument is grounded vpon thefe words of the Apoftle: *No man taketh this honour vnto himfelfe, but hee that is called of God as Aaron. Heb.5.* Secondly, the Leuiticall priefts ought to be furniſhed with knowledge, therefore the minifters of the new Teftament &c. The ground of this reafon is fet downe by the Prophet *Malachi* in this fort: *The priefts lippes ſhal preferue knowledge, and they ſhall feeke the Lawe at his mouth: for he is the meſſenger of the Lord of Hoftes. Mal.2.* You fee nowe, I hope, that an argument may be framed from the Leuiti-

call

call priefthood to the minifterie of the newe Teftament: if you doe not, you are ftarke blind: if you do,
confeffe your ignorance. Thirdly, the minifterie of
death and condemnation, and the minifterie of the
fpirite and righteoufneffe : that which fhould be a-
bolifhed, and that which remaineth, are things very farre and greatly different: yet an argument may
be drawē from the one to the other in this fort. The
lawe which was the minifterie of death, of condemnation , and which fhould be abolifhed, was glori-
ous:therefore the Gofpel which is the minifterie of
the fpirite and righteoufnes, and which remaineth,
is more glorious. This argument is , as the Logicians call it, *à comparatis :* and is foundly gathered out
of thefe wordes of the holy Apoftle : *If the miniſtra-*
tion of death was glorious, how ſhall not the miniſtration of
the ſpirit be more glorious? If the miniſterie of condemna-
tion was glorious , much more doth the miniſtration of
righteouſnes exceede in glory : if that which ſhould be abo-
liſhed was glorious, much more ſhall that which remaineth
be glorious. 2.Cor.3. What fay you nowe mafter *Pen-*
ry? doe you not perceiue by this I haue fet downe,
that an argument may be drawen very aptly from
one thing to another, wherein there is great diffimi-
litude:which are not twinnes, which are vnmatcheable ? if you doe , be wifer hereafter in the name of
God. Whether an argument may be drawen from
the ciuill magiftracie , fhall appeare in an other
place.

I. Penry.

And thus much I thought needefull generally to fet downe concerning
your maner of dealing: not that I woulde any way difgrace you, whom I
reuerence : for that is no part of mine intent, the Lord is my witneffe. Nay
I would be loth to let that fillable efcape mee, that might giue you, or any

els

els the leaſt occaſió in the world, to thinke that I cary any other heart towards you,then I ought to beare towards a reuerent learned man fearing
God. And howſoeuer, vnleſſe you alter your iudgement, I can neuer a-
gree with you in theſe points, becauſe I am aſſured, you ſwarue from the
trueth: Yet this diſagreement ſhall be ſo farre from making a breach of
that bond of loue,wherewith in the Lord I am tyed vnto you, that I doubt
not, but wee ſhall be at one in that day , when all of vs ſhall be at vnitie in
him that remaineth one and the ſelfe ſame for euer.

R. Some.

It is gently done of you:when you haue broken my
head,you giue me a plaiſter: but I refuſe your ſurge-
rie.You wil not,you ſay,diſgrace me: You reuerēce
me:Good words.A foule hooke vnder a faire bait.If
you reuerēce your friends on this faſhion,what ſhal
your enemies looke for ? *Philippides* cudgelled his
owne father.A mōſtrous ſonne.Being asked why he
did ſo,his anſwer was: he did it for loue:ſträge loue.
I will accompt ſomewhat better of your reuerence.
If I ſwarue from the trueth, as you aſſure your ſelfe,
you haue great reaſon to diſſent from me : Gods
trueth muſt be preferred: It is more excellent then
any creature : but if I haue any learning , you doe
*toto cœlo errare.*You are ſtrangely wide: for,you haue
ſet downe abſurd errours for cleare trueths , and
haue condemned ſure points of diuinitie for groſſe
errours. I ſee litle hope of agreement betweene you
and me in theſe particulars. I am reſolute in my
iudgement: if you be ſo in yours, I am ſory for you.
God giue you an other minde.

K.iii.   CHAP.

Iohn Penry.

Owe I am to come to your booke: from the 20. page whereof vnto the 28. laying the foundation of the reasons you vse against me, to proue the lawfulnesse of communicating with dumbe ministers, you handle two needelesse points. First, that they which were baptized by popish priests, haue receiued true baptisme as touching the substance. Secondly, that they are the Sacraments of baptisme, and the holy Supper of the Lord, which are deliuered in the Church of England by vnpreaching ministers. In these two points, M.*Some*, you haue proued nothing that my writings haue denied: but you haue quickened a dead controuersie, not vnlikely to giue the wrangling spirits of this age, cause to breede greater sturres in the Church. I see no other effect, which the handling of these questions can bring foorth but this. And it is to be feared that the slendernes of the reasons vsed in your booke, to proue that which you haue vndertaken to shew, will giue occasion vnto many, who of themselues are too too ready to iangle, to doubt of that whereof before they made no question. So that by seeking to stay the course of a needeful controuersie, you haue both giuen it a larger passage, and opened the doore vnto a question very fruitlesse in our time. You knowe I deale in neither of these pointes. If you cannot be stayed from entring into controuersies that are very odious, and more impertinent vnto the matter in hande: it were good that the Church were further and more soundly satisfied by you in these two points, which you alone in our Church haue publiquely called in question. And for mine owne part, when you haue done, I knowe not who will be your aduersarie: I see no reason why I shoulde deale in controuersies of so small gaine. Of this I am assured, that neither Popish priestes, nor any other ignorant guides are Ministers. Whether the Element administred by them, be a Sacramēt or no, looke you to that, which haue in your Treatise debated that, which my writings neuer called into question. If you will needes proue readers to be Ministers, because you cannot get mee to denie that which hath bene administred to be a Sacrament, you shall but presse that which will proue nothing. Your reason is, as if you should say, that either all they which supplie the places of ministers are ministers, or els an inconuenience is likely to followe. A strange maner of demonstration: Gods ordinance must needes be thrust out of the doores, because an inconuenience would be likely to ensue the admitting of it. The cause will not be thus answered at your hands, and I am sory that a man so reuerend in mine eyes, hath dealt so vnsubstantially, in a matter belonging to the seruice of the euerliuing God: the slendernesse of the reason is apparant. In the latter end of the booke I haue further shewed the same: thither I am to referre you and the reader.

R. Some.

R.Some.

You are come at the laſt to my treatiſe. In Gods name. You giue out that I dealt in two needeleſſe points. Not ſo, by your leaue: for ſome in London and other places, being ſeduced by vnſkilfull teachers, denied them both. You do not ſo, your words are as cleare as the day, and are theſe: *In theſe two poyntes M.Some &c. you haue proued nothing that my writings haue denied.* I thanke you for this. You are nowe in a very good moode: but you will not be ſo long. *Virtutes latere nõ poſſunt.* Ful veſſels wil burſt, if they haue not a vent. If you deny not that true baptiſme was deliuered by popiſh prieſtes and vnpreaching miniſters, you cannot deny popiſh prieſtes and vnpreaching miniſters to haue a calling. My reaſon is: *Nullum Sacramentum ſine miniſtro:* that is, No Sacrament without a miniſter. The wrangling ſpirits you write of, are the more becauſe of your abſurde writings: but they are not ſo many, thankes be to God, as you imagine. They which are ſo forwarde in iangling of theſe points, are either of your humour, which is very bad, or Anabaptiſticall recuſants, which is ſomewhat worſe. You adde theſe words, *A ſtrange manner of demonſtration* &c. They do proclaime your ignorance: they doe not anſwere my reaſon. I perceiue an argument *ab abſurdo,* is a pille that will not downe with you. The ſlendernes of my reaſons is repeated by you euery handwhile. It is like the Cuckoes ſong. It pleaſeth you againe to reuerence me. You are at more coſt then I would haue you. This reuerence is either a burden or a benefit. If a burden, lade ſome other with it: If a benefit, *beneficium non datur inuito,* I will none of it.

I. Penry.

Nowe I coulde well ouerpaſſe theſe two pointes, becauſe of themſelues they contayne nothing that I haue withſtoode : but in as much as you haue not onely grounded them vpon falſe principles, and ſuch as in no wiſe can be warranted by the Canon of the worde, but alſo inferre vpon their graunt, that our readers are miniſters, and conſequently that it is no ſinne to communicate with them : I am firſt to ſet downe the ſtate of the queſtion, which in deede is and ought to bee decided betweene you and me concerning the Element adminiſtred both by popiſh prieſtes, and other vnpreaching miniſters: and ſecondly to examine the grounds whereby you prooue the Element already deliuered by them to be a ſacrament, which you knowe I doe not deny to be ſo.

R. Some.

Becauſe I haue an ill memory, you tell me againe and againe, that you deny not the ſixth and ſeuenth propoſition of my treatiſe, It is well done of you. I would you woulde keepe you there. Onely you miſlike the foundatiõ I built on, and ſome conſequents. I am ſory for your heauineſſe. My grounds, you ſay, ſhalbe examined. Spare them not. Arraigne them if you will. But what ſhall I reaſon of, or looke for at your hands? To be acquited? no hope of that. To be condemned? It is certaine: for, it hath pleaſed you to giue ſentence before examination. Harde dealing: but I muſt abide it.

I. Penry.

The queſtion therefore is not whether the one or the other of them haue deliuered a Sacrament in reſpect of the action done, but whether a Chriſtian going vnto them for thoſe holy ſeales, may be aſſured, that hee can receiue the ſame at their hands. I affirme that wee cannot: *M. Some* taketh it graunted that we may. My warrant is out of the worde, becauſe there is no promiſe made to vs therein, that the action celebrated by ſuch men, is a Sacramentall action: and where there is no promiſe, there can be no aſſurance, becauſe our aſſurance ariſeth onely of faith, which muſt be grounded vpon the promiſes ſette downe in the worde. We haue no promiſe that they can deliuer vs a Sacrament, becauſe they are no miniſters. For they onely are enioyned by our Sauiour Chriſt to deliuer a Sacrament, neither doe we knowe what he can deliuer which is no miniſter.

R.Some.

No maruaile though you diſſent from me.*Conue-niet nulli,qui ſecum &c.*You are at warre with your ſelfe. Your wordes agree like harpe and harrowe. One while,you denie not that popiſh prieſtes and vnpreaching miniſters haue deliuered a ſacrament: An other while you knowe not what they can deli-uer: for,they are,as you ſay,no miniſters. To that ende you depraue Chriſts ſpeech in S.Matthew &c. What dealing is this? Sacrament, and no Sacra-ment,and all with one breath? What? can ſuch as are no miniſters, deliuer a Sacrament? If you ſay, No:then popiſh Prieſtes & vnpreaching miniſters, neither haue nor can deliuer a Sacrament: for they are,as you ſay,no miniſters, that is, they haue no calling at all.Your diſciples are fit veſſels to receiue any liquor of yours: but men of learning and wiſe-dome,are otherwiſe affected.They ſee clearely,that your dealing is abſurde and dangerous. Abſurde: for it is voyde of trueth. Dangerous: for it woulde breede confuſion. The magiſtrates, thankes bee to God,neither doe nor will ſuffer this bad courſe of yours. If they ſhould, fancies woulde (as weedes) growe too too faſt,and this noble land ſhoulde re-ceiue more hurt then your head is worth. I doubt not of their godly wiſdome. The miſerable eſtate of *Germanie* heretofore, by reaſon of Sectaries, may and will awake them. If you be reſtrained for your groſſe errours, as ſome other are very iuſtly: you may not cry, perſecution, perſecution: your note muſt be *pœna perfidiæ*, that is, that you are iuſtly met with.Otherwiſe you ſing out of tune.

L.   *I.Penry.*

I. Penry.

So that the queſtion is now growen to this iſſue, Whether Popiſh prieſts and our vnpreaching Miniſters, be Miniſters or no: whom if I can proue to bee none, then the matter is cleare, that no man going vnto them for the Sacrament, can aſſure himſelfe there to haue the ſame. And this ſhall be a generall reaſon, equally belonging vnto both the pointes handled by you, the particulers whereof ſhall follow in their places.

R. Some.

If you can proue that, I will commende and pre-ferre you before *Martyr, Bucer, Caluine, Beza*, and o-ther very famous men and Churches. Yea, I will de-nie her Maieſtie and a great number of her excel-lent ſubiects to bee baptized, which I am ſure are baptized. The marke you leuell at, is (as I take it) ei-ther to ſend many thouſands to the Font againe, or to make them guiltie of contempt of Baptiſme. One of theſe two muſt needes fall out, if Popiſh prieſtes, and vnpreaching Miniſters (without any calling) did adminiſter a Sacrament. You may leuell and le-uell againe at this marke : but you ſhall neuer hit it. The Bowe you ſhoote in, is too ſtrong: and your armes are very weake. Beſides, you would faine haue me confeſſe that either Popiſh prieſts and ignorant Miniſters, are lawfull and good Miniſters of God: or that no Sacrament was or is deliuered by them. I will graunt you neither. Not the firſt, for I abhorre that defence: Not the ſecond, for I deteſt your Ana-baptiſticall fancies. The next thing you deale in, is, that neither Popiſh prieſtes nor vnpreaching Mini-ſters are miniſters. In which Treatiſe you bewray in-tollerable both pride and ignorance. What I like or miſlike in that diſcourſe, appeareth in the end of this booke. Thither I referre you. I will now ſet downe that part of my Treatiſe which you fight againſt.

C H A P.

THEY WHICH WERE

baptized in the Popish Church by Popish Priestes, receiued true Baptisme, touching the substance of Baptisme.

R.Some.

He Popish priestes doe retaine the essentiall forme of Christes baptisme, that is, they doe baptize in the name, not of Pope or idole, but of the holy Trinitie: therefore it is not mans, but Gods baptisme, which is deliuered by them. If it be Gods baptisme, I am sure it is true baptisme. Master *Caluin* calleth them Catabaptists, which denie that we are rightly baptized in the Popish Church. *Institut.lib.4.cap.15.Sect.16.*

I.Penry.

Nowe to the examination of your reason brought to prooue that they which were baptized in Poperie, haue receiued true baptisme. Your conclusion, you must remember, I doe not denie, though your reason proueth not the same, which is thus framed. Whosoeuer deliuer Gods baptisme, they deliuer true baptisme: But Popish priestes deliuer Gods baptisme, therefore true baptisme. You haue changed the conclusion from that which was done, vnto that which is done: But this ouersight I omit. The assumption you proue thus: Whosoeuer baptize in the name not of Pope or Idols, but of the holy Trinitie, they deliuer Gods baptisme: but Popish priestes doe baptize in the name of the holy Trinitie, therefore they deliuer Gods baptisme. Your proposition in this last Sillogisme is most false, and such as vpon the grant whereof, not onely the communicating with vnpreaching ministers might be adouched, but also Gods whole ordinance in the institution of his holy Sacraments quite ouerthrowen. For if it were true, that there were no more required to make substantiall baptisme (as you here require no more) but to baptize in the name of the Trinitie: then these impious absurdities would followe thereof. 1 That an Amalekite might deliuer true circumcision, as touching the substance. 2 That true baptisme might be administred vnto a substance not capable of baptisme: But this odious instance I will not vrge. 3. That a woman, 4. That any man not being a Minister, as a childe of fiue yeeres olde, a Turke, or Iewe, might deliuer true baptisme as touching the substance. For

these

thefe pronouncing the words of Inftitution, might retaine, by your reafon the effentiall forme of Chrifts baptifme, and fo to vfe your owne wordes, they baptizing not in the name of Pope or of Idols, but of the holy Trinitie, fhould deliuer Gods baptifme and not mans? If Gods baptifme, then true baptifme I am fure: in like maner, by this reafon they fhould be Catabaptifts, which denie men to be rightly baptized by Turkes or women.

R.*Some.*

You denie not my conclufion. I muft you fay remember it. You haue fung this fong very often. It needed not, A worde had bene ynough if it had fo pleafed you. You tell me, You wil omit an ouerfight of mine. You deferue no thankes for this courtefie: therefore I will giue you none. But what I befeeche you is my ouerfight? Forfooth, I doe accompt it as true baptifme, which is adminiftred now as heretofore in the Popifh Church. Call you this an ouerfight? Was it true baptifme yefterday and is it none to day? A marueilous cafe: This is like thofe abfurde fellowes, of whome *Tertullian* writeth in an other cafe: *Hodie presbyter, qui cras laicus. De prefcr.aduerfus Hær.* That is, to day a Minifter, but to morow none. You are one of the ftrageft Diuines that euer I hard of. Very ignorant: very bould: very abfurde. You are fuch a one as the Apoftle mentioneth, *1.Tim.1.7.* To proceede: my reafon you fay prooueth not my propofition. In the iudgement of any learned man it doeth: if not in yours, the matter is not great: for your iudgement is not worth a rufh. The argumēt I made is in deede *M.Caluines,* & a very fure one. It is allowed of all Churches, that I can heare of. It pleafeth you to fet downe my reafon thus: Whofoeuer deliuer Gods baptifme, they deliuer true baptifme: But Popifh priefts deliuer Gods baptifme, therfore true baptifme. You fay I proue my Minor thus:

Who-

Whofoeuer baptize in the name not of Pope or i-
dols,but of the holy Trinity,they deliuer Gods bap-
tifme.But Popifh prieftes &c. Your anfwere is that
my Maior propofitiō is moft falfe, & that vpon the
grant of it, many abfurdities would folow,&c.Your
dealing with mee is moft abfurde. It fhall appeare
thus.My Minor propofition fet downe by you,was:
Popifh priefts deliuer Gods baptifme. You fay I
proue it thus : Whofoeuer baptize in the name not
of Pope or idols,but of the holy Trinitie, they deliuer Gods baptifme.Vpō this you inferre many cōfe-
fequēts at your pleafure: viz.that Turkes,Iewes,wo-
men,priuate men,children, might deliuer true baptifme touching the fubftance. You pretende great
finceritie. Anfwere mee directly. I appeale to your
confcience,if you haue any. Did I euer deliuer fuch
a Maior propofition? If I haue, quote the page, fet
downe the words. If I haue not, (which I am wel affured of)you haue grofly abufed me.You may as eafily fetch oyle out of a flint,as any fuch confequents
out of my writings.The godly reader may fee by this
litle, howe neere you are driuen, when you vfe fuch
beggerly fhifts to bumbaft your Treatife. Honeft
Matrones vfe no painting : but harlots doe, Simple
trueth needes no lies to welt and gard it : groffe errours haue neede of fuch Vermilion. They which
haue either heard my Sermōs, or read my writings,
doe knowe very well,that I allowe none whatfoeuer
without a calling, to adminifter a Sacrament or
preach the word, therefore neither woman nor priuate man. Yea, mine owne wordes in this prefent
chapter are as cleare as the funne: viz.Popifh priefts
doe retaine the effentiall forme of Chriftes bap-

tifme,&c.which Popifh priefts haue a calling thogh
a faultie one. It is very ftrãge that you could not fee
this. I perceiue,the vaile of malice did hinder your
fight. The odious inftance you mention, doeth beft
become your Spirit. It is futable to the reft of your
writings,that is,moft abfurd and childifh.

I.Penry.

I would be fulfory, that the errours of the Catabaptifts or Anabaptifts,
coulde not bee confuted by you with founder reafons, then this you haue
brought: and I would be alfo fory, that you fhoulde defende fuch abfurd
confequents as I wil driue you vnto whether you will or no,vnleffe you re-
uoke(as I hope you will) that which you haue written. Pardon me, I pray
you. I deale as reuerently as I may with you, retayning the maieftie of the
caufe I defend,and I deale not againft you,but againft an erroneous affertion, which I now leaue: defiring you very earneftly, that you would confider howe vnreuerently the ordinance of God in the holy Sacraments is
dealt with, when the fame is made to depende vpon the pronouncing of a
few fillables, without any confideration either of the perfon who is to adminifter,or of the fubftantial forme of confecration conteined in the ex-
pofition of the holy inftitution of baptifme,& the inuocation of the Name
of God, all which are neceffarily required in the adminiftration of baptifme,and could not poffibly be in _Egypt_,where all was and is couered vnder the darkenes of a ftrange tongue.

R.Some.

You pretend great forrow for me.I do not thanke
you for it.Be forie for your owne abfurdities,which
are many & groffe. The abfurde confequents which
you will driue me perforce vnto, vnleffe I reuerfe
my writings, are eafily numbred.They are not one,
thankes be to God.Your lufty fpeech can not daunt
me. It is but a vifour. I haue bene long acquainted
with the boyfterous fpeeches of fuch ignorant and
bolde companions as you are. Touching the argument nowe in hand betweene vs,fpare me not: I defire no fauour: I will not reuoke any iot I haue fet
downe.You defire pardon of me.If you recant your
Anabaptifticall errours,you fhall haue an eafie fuit:
Otherwife,

Otherwife,I do and wil account verie bafely of you.
Hath the caufe you deale for , Maieftie in it ? You
might haue fpared the name of Maieftie verie well.
It is too coftly a garment for fuch a leprous body,as
your Treatife is. But I muft beare with you. It is the
maner of Sectaries to vfe maiefticall & loftie words,
that their ignorant followers may commend them
aboue the skies. The reuerend dealing you talke of,
is idle fpeech. I haue and doe refufe it. The erroni-
ous affertion which you fight againft, is not mine: I
did neuer fo much as once thinke of it. It is yours:
vfe it as you lift.You may be bolde with it.You giue
out, that I make the Sacrament to depend vpon the
pronouncing of a fewe fillables, without confideration of the perfon who is to adminifter it. My
anfwere is,that you are a wicked flaunderer.You require three things neceffarily in the adminiftration
of baptifme. Firft, one which hath calling to adminifter it. I agree with you in this. Secondly,the fubftantiall forme of confecration conteined in the ex-
pofition of the holy inftitution of Baptifme.I diffent
from you in this, and yet doe like found preaching
as well as you. Laftly, the inuocation of the name
of God. I fay Amen to this. Then you adde this Minor: but thefe could not poffibly be in *Egypt,*that is,
in the Popifh Church,&c.Will you ftand to the fecond branch of the three ? If you doe, I may iuftly
conclude , firft that you account *Confecration*, not
Chrifts words in baptifme,as you ought , but fome
gloffe vpon Chriftes wordes,which you ought not:
Secondly, that you denie any Sacrament to be deliuered by Popifh Priefts, & vnpreaching Minifters,
&c, And yet you haue faid often, and haue defired

mee to remember that you denie it not. I doe not wring your wordes, and pull them out of ioynt, as you doe mine. Such dealing is an argument of a vile nature and wrangling spirit. It is verie farre, I thanke God, from me : I doe detest it. If I were of your humour, I could chase and pursue you hotly, for your inconstancie & errour: Inconstancie, for affirming and denying one and the selfe same particular : Errour, for giuing out that the worde preached is necessarily required to the Essence of the Sacrament. If a sermon were necessarily required to the Essence of a Sacrament, these absurdities woulde followe : First, the Sacraments are dead Sacraments, that is, seales without writing, and plaine blankes, if there vvant a sermon: Secondly, if Baptisme be no sacrament vvithout a sermon, then can it not regenerate or bee effectuall to any vvhich either haue bene, or are baptized vvithout a sermon.

Obiection of the fantasticall crew.

The Popish Priests haue no lawfull calling : therfore it is no true Baptisme which is deliuered by them.

R. Some.

The Argument followes not. I confesse that Popish priests haue no lawfull calling : yet they haue a calling, though a faultie one. They which are not lawfully called vnto the ministery, are to be accounted in another place then they which haue no calling *Caiphas* was not in deed the lawfull high Priest : for he entred by money, and the Priesthood in his time was rent in pieces : yet becaufe hee sate in the high Priestes chaire, hee was accounted the high Priest. A faultie vocation may hurt him that vsurpes an office, but it doeth not defile those thinges which are done by that partie. This is M. *Bezaes* iudgement

iudgement in his 142.queſtion.

If any ſhall gather of this, that I allow the Popiſh Prieſthoode, he deſerues rather a cenſor, then confuter. For I confeſſe, that *Sacerdotium Papiſticum eſt ſacrilegium :* that is, that the Popiſh Prieſthoode is Sacriledge.

I.Penry.

Your diſtinction that Popiſh Prieſtes haue a calling, though a faultie, is a begging of the queſtion. For as I haue ſhewed, Popiſh Prieſts haue no calling at all in the Church, and therefore howe can they ſit in the chaire of the miniſterie? Is there a miniſterie out of the Church? Caiphas prieſthood commeth afterward to be conſidered of.

R.Some.

The diſtinction vvhich you ſay is mine, is in deed M. *Bezaes.* It is tearmed by you a begging of the queſtion. Nay rather, your anſwere to M. *Beʒa* is beggerly, and none at all. If Popiſh prieſts (as you write) haue no calling at all : firſt, *Luther,* which had impoſition of handes in the Popiſh Church, had no externall calling at all: Secondly, in your iudgement, either no Baptiſme was deliuered by Popiſh Prieſts in the Popiſh Church: or, Baptiſme, if any were in the Popiſh Church, was adminiſtred by priuate men : for they which haue no calling at all, are priuate men. I neede not driue you to abſurde conſequents : you caſt your ſelfe headlong into them, as into a dangerous quauemire. Your Treatiſes wherein you haue ſowen groſſe errours thicke and threefolde, are witneſſes ynough of this. Are not your diſciples moſt vnhappie, which depende on you as on another Pope ? You aske whether there is a miniſtery out of the Church. What my iudgemēt is, appeareth hereafter. In the meane time, you deny not, that there is true baptiſme (therefore conſequently a mi-

M.　　　　　　niſtery)

niftery) in the Popifh Church which (you fay) is no
Church. *Caiphas* Priefthoode hath both fearched
and founde you out. It bewrayeth your groffe ignorance.

CHAP. 8.

THEY ARE THE SACRA-

*ments of Baptifme and the holy Supper, which
are deliuered in the Church of England, by vn=
preaching Minifters.*

I.Penry.

Ou knowe M.*Some*, what I meane by an vnpreaching
Minifter, namely euery one, learned or vnlearned,
that cannot fhewe himfelfe by the good triall of his
giftes, to haue that fitneffe to teach, whereof we read
2.Tim.2. 1.Tim.3. Which abilitie the Lord doeth not
ordinarily beftow vpon any in thefe our dayes, without the knowledge of the Artes, efpecially the two
handmaides of all learning, Rhetoricke, and Logique, and the two origi-
nall tongues wherein the worde was written.

R.Some.

If none are to be accounted minifters ordinarily,
which are not furnifhed, as you prefcribe and require : many in the primitiue Church after Chriftes
Afcenfion were no ordinarie minifters : *Valerius* a
godly man, whom *Auguftine* fucceeded at *Hippo* in
Afrique, was no ordinarie minifter. *Poffid. in vita
Aug.cap.5.* Sam*fucius*, a godly Bifhop, was no ordinarie minifter. *Aug.epift. 168. Auguftine*, which
was a famous man, was no ordinarie minifter. Many
profitable paftours in this age, are no ordinarie minifters. Yea, M.*Penryes* ignorant Leuiticall prieftes,
whome hee alloweth and defendeth to bee lawfull
Priefts, were no ordinarie minifters.

R.*Some.*

R.Some.

If ſuch as were baptized in the popiſh Church, receiued true baptiſme, I truſt they are rightly baptized in the Church of England, which are baptized by vnpreaching miniſters.

I. Penry.

The reſt of your booke is now to be examined.Your coucluſion,pag.22. that they which were baptized by vnpreaching miniſters, are rightly baptized as touching the ſubſtance of baptiſme, I doe not gaineſay. Your reaſons are weake : for howe could we proue your concluſion, if men ſhoulde denie popiſh baptiſme,to be true baptiſme,as I doe not,you knowe, and he ſhould doe me great iniurie , which would lay that to my charge. Were it ſufficient for vs to ſay they were Catabaptiſts which denie popiſh baptiſme ? howe coulde this be proued ? and this ſhoulde not proue the matter doubted of.

R.Some.

Do you anſwere of this faſhion? this is as farre off, as *Yorke* from *London*. The ſumme of your anſwere is, that my reaſons are weake, & that you denie not my concluſion. Are my reaſons weake,becauſe you ſay ſo? If they were like your ſenſeles anſweres, they were ſtrange ſtuffe. If you deny not the, which were baptized by vnpreaching miniſters , to be rightly baptized: it is a neceſſarie conſequent,euen in your owne iudgement: firſt, that either vnpreaching miniſters are miniſters, or that priuate men may deliuer a Sacrament: ſecondly , that it was and is a Sacrament, which is adminiſtred without a Sermon. They which denie that ſuch as were baptized in the popiſh Church, receiued true baptiſme, touching the ſubſtance of baptiſme , are Catabaptiſts in the iudgement of all learned writers and reformed Churches.I reſt in their iudgement.

R.Some.

If ſuch as were baptized by popiſh prieſts in the
M.ij.   popiſh

popifh Church, and by vnpreaching minifters in the Church of England, receiued no Sacrament, many groffe abfurdities would followe. Firft, very many are vnbaptized : and if they be vnbaptized, they finne grieuoufly, in not prefenting themfelues to the holy Sacrament.

I. Penry.

Shall we fay that they finne, in not prefenting themfelues to be baptized? fo whom fhould they prefent themfelues? who would baptize them?

R. Some.

What meane fcholer in either of the Vniuerfities? yea, what Ruffet coate in the Countrey would fhape fuch an anfwere? In fteade of anfwering my reafons, you aske me two queftions: I muft be content to anfwere, there is no remedie. Your firft queftion is : Shall we fay that they finne in not prefenting themfelues to be baptized? My anfwere is: they doe finne : no learned and godly man doubtes of it: my reafons are: Firft, Baptifme is *externus charaƈter*, that is, the outward marke and badge of a Chriftian: fo writeth that famous man M. *Foxe, Cap. 14.* in *Apocal.* Secondly, the contempt of circumcifion was grieuoufly punifhed, *Gen. 17.* Yea, the Angel would haue killed *Mofes*, becaufe his fonne was not circumcifed, *Exod. 4.* Thirdly, they in the primitiue Church which had excellent graces, prefented themfelues to baptifme: which baptifme before, they had not. So did many in *Ierufalem* after *Peters* fermon, *Aƈt. 2.* many in *Samaria* after *Philips* fermons, *Aƈt. 8.* many in *Corinth* after *Pauls* fermons, *Aƈt. 18.* Your fecond queftion is: to whom fhould they prefet them felues: who would baptize them? my anfwere is: after a publique profeffion of their faith in the chriftian

ftian affembly, they muft prefent themfelues to be
baptized of the minifter. So did *Cornelius* in *Cafarea,*
Act.10. Lidia in *Philippi, Acts.16. Crifpus* and *Gaius* in
*Corinth. Act.18.1.Cor.1.*and a Iewe of late yeeres in
*London.*I fpeake nowe of fuch as be of yeres, and are
vnbaptized. I hope you wil not gather of this, that I
fhut our infants from the holy Sacrament of Baptifme: if you fhould, you deferue rather to be cen-
fured by the Magiftrate, then to be confuted by argument.

R. Some.

If fuch as were baptized by popifh priefts in the
popifh Church, and by vnpreaching minifters in
the Church of *England* receiued no Sacrament, a
great number haue finned grofly in partaking the
holy Supper. My reafon is: none vncircumcifed
might eate the Paffeouer, *Exo.12.48.*therefore none
vnbaptized, may receiue the holy Supper.

I.Penry.

Admit they finned in receiuing the Lords Supper, before they were
baptized, fhould they therefore be bereaued of the comfort of baptifme?
to affirme that this were a going backward, is no reafon, becaufe they were
perfwaded that they had baptifme, otherwife they would not haue bene fo
farre on their iourney, vntill they had bene accompanied therewith: But
they omitted baptifme of ignorance, and not of contempt: therefore they
denie the receiuing of the Lords Supper, to haue bene a finne any more,
then it would be a finne in them nowe to receiue the Lords Supper, if they
could not haue Baptifme. Baptifme they would haue, if they could orderly
come by the fame. Becaufe men wil be fo iniurious vnto them, as to deny them the comfort of baptifme, which they cannot haue, fhoulde they
denie to themfelues the comfort of the Lordes Supper which they may
haue? Yea, but no vncircumcifed might eate the pafeal lambe.*Exod.*12.48
True: But what fhall we fay vnto thofe that were vncircumcifed in the wilderneffe fortie yeeres almoft? *Iof.5.5.* Did they neuer eate the paffeouer all that time? If they did, the place of *Exodus* will be quickly anfwered.
It is plaine that the paffeouer was celebrated in the wilderneffe once at
the leaft *Nom.9.1.* If euery yeere, why fhould the godly of the familie bee
excluded from the action, the caufe why they were vncircumcifed not
being in them?

M.iij. *R.Some.*

R.*Some.*

You anſwere very ſtrangely. Your wittes, I thinke, were a wooll gathering. If they ſinned in partaking the Lordes ſupper before they were baptized, there is great reaſon they ſhoulde abſtaine from the holy table, vntill they bee baptized : which Baptiſme (if the caſe ſo required) might orderly and eaſily bee come by. But they omitted baptiſme, you ſay, of ignoraunce, not of contempt: therefore they ſinned not , which being vnbaptized did partake the holy Supper. I denie your argument : My reaſon is : *Ignorátia excuſat non à toto, ſed à tanto :* that is, Ignorance maketh the fault leſſe, it doth not make it none. M. *Penry* at the length toucheth one part of my reaſon: but by his leaue I will firſt ſet downe my whole reaſon, and then his anſwere. My reaſon is this: None vncircumciſed might eat the paſſeouer. *Exod.12.48.* therefore, none vnbaptized may receiue the holy Supper. M. *Penryes* anſwere is conteined in theſe wordes: True, But what ſhall we ſay vnto thoſe that were vncircumciſed in the wilderneſſe fortie yeeres almoſt. *Ioſua.5.5.* Did they neuer eate the Paſſeouer all that time ? If they did, the place of *Exodus* will be quickely anſwered. It is plaine that the Paſſeouer was celebrated in the wilderneſſe once at the leaſt. *Nombers 9.1.* If euery yeere, why ſhoulde the godly of the familie bee excluded from the action , the cauſe why they were vncircumciſed not being in them ? Call you this anſwering? There was neuer any ſuch I am ſure in *Cambridge* or *Oxford.* It came I thinke out of *Barbarie.* I hope you are aſhamed of it by this time. You aske mee whether they which were vncircumciſed in the wilderneſſe almoſt fortie

yeeres,

yeeres, did all that time neuer eate the Paſſeouer?
My anſwere is, that no ſuch thing appeareth in the
text: and where the holy Ghoſt ſtayeth his penne, it
becommeth vs to ſtay our tongues. Yea, it is cleare
in *Ioſue*, that the Iſraelites, after they were circumciſed, did keepe the feaſt of the Paſſeouer. *Ioſ.ſ.8.10*.
You adde, If the Iſraelites being vncircumciſed, did
partake the Paſſeouer, that the place in *Exodus* will
be quickely anſwered. You ſay true. If the skie fall,
you ſhall catch Larkes. When you proue this (*if*) of
yours, I wil accept your anſwere. Till then, you ſhal
pardon me. You proceed in this ſort, It is plaine you
ſay that the Paſſeouer was celebrated in the wilderneſſe, once at the leaſt, *Numb.9*. Will you conclude
of this : therefore they which were vncircumciſed
did eate the Paſſeouer? If you doe, I denie your argument : My reaſon is: If they had admitted any vncircumciſed to the Paſſeouer, they had prophaned
the holy Sacrament. The wordes in the text are manifeſt : *If a ſtranger dwell with thee, and will obſerue the*
Paſſeouer of the Lord, let him circumciſe all the males, that
belong vnto him, and then let him come and obſerue it, and
he ſhall bee as one that is borne in the lande : for, no vncir-
cumciſed perſon ſhall eate thereof. One lawe ſhall bee to him
that is borne in the land, and to the ſtranger that dwelleth
among you. Exod.12. An other reaſon of yours is : the
cauſe why the Iſraelites were vncircumciſed, was
not in them : therefore the godly vncircumciſed of
the family might not be barred from the Paſſeouer.
I anſwere : your argument is naught, and verie ſaw-
cie : for, you comptroll Almightie God by whome
they were barred. This is no pride, M.*Penry*. I might
ſay to you as the Apoſtle in another caſe : *O man, who*

art thou that pleadeſt againſt God? hath not the potter power of the Clay,&c.Rom.9. I confeſſe that the Iſraelites ceaſed from circumciſion in the wildernes: and yet were not faultie in omitting and deferring circumciſion: for, they had Gods ſpeciall diſpenſation to do ſo, becauſe they were in côtinuall trauaile: and people being newly circumciſed, could abide no labour. For the ſurer proofe of this point: vidz. that none which are knowen to bee vnbaptized, may either preſent themſelues, or be admitted to the holy Supper, I offer theſe reaſons to the godly Reader. Firſt, Baptiſme is an entrâce into the viſible church: the holy Supper is a confirmation of this entrance. Secondly, they which were of yeeres in the primitiue Church were firſt baptized, and afterwarde receiued the holy Supper. This is manifeſt in theſe wordes of S. *Luke : Then they that gladly receyued his worde, were baptized: and the ſame day, there were added to the Church about three thouſand ſoules. And they continued in the Apoſtles doctrine and fellowſhip, and breaking of bread and prayers, &c. Act.2.* By *breaking of bread,* is vnderſtanded the partaking of the Lords Supper. Thirdly, None may preſent themſelues to the holy table, before due examination of themſelues. *1.Cor. 11.* This examination conſiſteth of faith and repentance : which faith and repentance are not in them, which either wittingly omit, or wilfully contemne the holy Sacrament of baptiſme: which baptiſme is the Sacrament of repentance. *Matth.3.Calu. Inſt.lib.4.cap.19.ſect.17.* Laſtly, all famous men and Churches are of my ſide. If maiſter *Penry* diſſent, it is no great matter. His writings are not as the lawes of the *Medes* and *Perſians, &c.*

R. *Some.*

If fuch as vvere baptized by popifh Priefts in the popifh Church,and by vnpreaching minifters in the Church of England, receiued no Sacrament, many excellent men haue vfurped the preachers office. My reafon is: It is vnlawful for any man to be a publique teacher in the vifible Church, which is not by baptifme graft into,and fo become a member of the vifible Church. Our Sauiour Chrift was baptized of *Iohn* in Iordane before he preached. *Mat.3.* and *4.Chap.*The Apuftle *Paule* was baptized of *Ananias* in *Damafcus,*before he preached. *Act.9.*

None vncircumcifed might minifter before the altar. True : but did none of the Leuites that were borne in the wildernes,teach *Iacob* the law, or offer the incenfe of his God in all thofe forty yeeres ?

The truth I perceiue, is mightie. It maketh the enemie many times to confeffe it: fo doth it you in this place, Your wordes are cleare for me, and flat againft your felfe. You grant that none vncircumcifed might minifter before the altar, I thanke you for it. Of this I conclude : therefore none vnbaptized may be a publique teacher in the vifible church. Thus, you fee by the way,which may not be forgotten, that an argument may bee drawen from the Leuiticall priefthood to the minifterie of the newe teftament: which priefthood and minifterie are not twinnes,are vnmatcheable and cannot ftand together. I confeffe my felfe greatly bound vnto you: you deale very liberally with me : for you reach me arguments (as weapons)to fmite your felfe withall. *M. Penry* a little after in fteede of anfwering my reafon,asketh a queftion after his vfuall manner. Did (faith he) none of the vncircumcifed Leuites teach *Iacob* the lawe,or offer incenfe, &c.I anfwere : Firft, that no fuch thing appeareth in the text: Secondly, that it is againft the practife of the Leuiticall priefts in the olde Teftament.Did euer any ftudent deale fo childifhly, as M. *Penry* doth? is not he a very fit man to cenfure famous men & Churches? *Caluine, Martyr, Beza, Auguftine,&c.* are no body with him. I did neuer fee him that I knowe of : but , *ex vnguibus leonem:* I fee by his anfweres what a deepe clarke he is.

I. Penry.

Thus many things,you fee,might be obiected againft your reafons,and I take the obiections to be of fome waight. It had bene well, you had confidered of them,before you had publifhed your booke. And the Baptifme by vnpreaching minifters , muft haue better proofes , then any you haue brought as yet, or els I feare me, our pofterities will not be fatisfied therewith.

R. Some.

Your wayghtie obiections are inuincible in your eye. *Suum cuique pulchrum.* But they haue neither *Succum* nor *Sanguinem :* they haue no pith in them: they are lighter then any feather, and bewray your ignorance. You wifh I had confidered before hand of your obiections: *Satis pro imperio.*You are by your leaue a litle too lordly : had I nothing to thinke of but of your abfurde fancies ? you imagine very bafely of me. My arguments for baptifme by vnpreaching minifters are fuch , as you are vnable to ftirre: for proofe of this,I referre the reader to your vnfcholerlike anfweres. Your feare that the pofteritie will not reft in my reafons, is a vaine feare, &c.

R. Some.

The vnpreaching minifters doe adde the worde vnto the Element in the adminiftration of Baptifme : therefore it is the Sacrament of Baptifme which is deliuered by them. *Accedit verbum ad Elementum, & fit Sacramentum.* '*Auguft. Tract. 80.* in *Iohan.* that is, The worde is added to the Element, and it becomes a Sacrament. By *(worde)* in Baptifme is vnderftanded the worde of Inftitution, which is, to baptize in the name of the Father, the Sonne, and the holy Ghoft, &c. Of this iudgement are *Beza confeff. Cap. 4. Art. 47.* and *Mufculus de fig. Sacram. Art. 4.*

I. Penry.

Your next reafon, page 23. is flender. Readers pronounce the wordes of Inftitution with the deliuerie of the Element, therefore (fay you) they deliuer a Sacrament. You haue once already alledged this to prooue popifh baptifme, page 20. I haue anfwered it page 29. 30. 31. And the place of *Matth.* 28.19. brought in by you page 23. prooueth your confequent to bee falfe. For it fheweth, that hee, who is to baptize, muft bee alfo able to teache, which abilitie is wanting in our Readers. *Goe*, fayth our Sauiour, *and teache all nations, baptizing &c.* Therefore if hee, that deliuereth the Element, be not able to teache, we cannot be affured, that it is a Sacrament: Becaufe the commaundement is not generally to all that coulde pronounce the wordes of Inftitution, being thereunto permitted by the corruption of the time, but particularly limitted vnto them that can teache, vnleffe you will fay that the Lorde biddeth them goe teache, who cannot teache : which were not once to bee conceiued of his Maieftie.

R. Some.

Whatfoeuer paffeth from me is flender in your opinion. All that you deliuer, is *ex tripode,* an oracle

at the leaſt. You anſwered before wiſely & like your
ſelfe. So you doe in this place: *ſemper idem*: you are
no changeling. You deny my conſequent, and doe
adde for your reaſon an obiection ſet downe by me
a litle after. My anſwere to that obiection is extant
and very direct. I reſt in it: I did neuer ſay or thinke
that Almightie God did either command or allow
any to be a prieſt in the old, or a miniſter in the new
Teſtament, which had not gifts in ſome meaſure. It
pleaſeth you to write in your treatiſe, that vnfitnes
to teach made not a nullitie of the Leuiticall prieſts
office. Ifyou meane, that it made not a nullitie before God, you conceiue very baſely of Almightie
God: for, you make him to allowe ignorant men to
be his prieſts in the olde Teſtament: which abſurde
courſe would haue brought great diſhonour to his
Maieſtie, and great hurt to the Church of the Iſraelites. I doe nowe but touch this groſſe and blaſphemous paradoxe of yours: and (with the dog of E-
gypt) doe, as it were, ſippe and away: but I will examine it more ſurely hereafter, that the reader may
ſee clearely, as in a Chriſtall glaſſe, what baſe ware
you commend vnto vs for excellent diuinitie.

I. Penry.

The corruption in the Church of Englande, that the deliuerie of the
Element ſhoulde be ſeuered from the preaching of the worde, is a breach
of Gods ordinance, you cannot deny, *Matth.28.19. Actes 20.7.* and therefore vngodly and intollerable. Whether it make the action fruſtrate or no,
that is not the queſtion.

R. Some.

You meane, as I take it, by the worde added to the
Element, the worde preached: but you doe not ſay
flatly

flatly here(though you haue a little before) that the
want of a Sermon maketh the action fruſtrate , that
is, the ſacrament to be no ſacrament.I confeſſe that
Paul preached at *Troas* in the adminiſtration of the
holy Supper, *Act.20.7.* and that the Apoſtles did
teach the Gentiles before they baptized them, *Mat.
28.19.*But no learned man will conclude of this,that
a Sermon is ſimplie neceſſarie to the Eſſence of a
Sacrament. If you will know,what I thinke of ſound
preaching before the adminiſtration of the holy ſa-
cramēt,my anſwer is,that I do greatly both like and
commend it. Yea,I doe wiſh with all my heart, that
all the Churches in Englande had able teachers to
performe that dutie. This minde was I euer of,ſince
I knewe what Gods religion and good diuinitie
meant.   Of this minde are all godly and learned
men in the Church of England.

An obiection of the fantaſticall ſort.

Chriſt ſayde to his Apoſtles, Goe and teach all nations, baptizing &c.
*Matt.*28.19.Therefore,if the worde preached, bee not added to the Element,it is no ſacrament of Baptiſme.

Anſwere.

The Argument is verie weake. I confeſſe, that
Chriſt cōmanded his Apoſtles, firſt to teach ſuch as
were of yeres and aliens from his religion,and then
to baptize them. If the Gentiles had not bene firſt
taught, they woulde not haue offered themſelues,
nor the Apoſtles admitted them to the holy ſacrament of Baptiſme. If any will conclude of this place
in ſaint *Matthewe,* that none whatſoeuer may be admitted to baptiſme,before they be taught:they ſhut
our infants from the holy ſacrament, and therefore
are Catabaptiſts.

Mafter *Penry* anfweres nothing to this. So am I eafed of fome labour.

R.*Some.*

The vnpreaching Minifters do adde *(verbum ædificans)* that is, an edifying word, to the Elements, in the adminiftratiõ of the holy Supper: therefore, &c.

I.*Penry.*

Vnpreaching Minifters doe adde an edifying worde vnto the Element, therfore it is a Sacrament. This reafon is the fame with the former. Which fheweth the great nakednes & pouertie of the caufe, that one reafon muft be thrife periured to proue the goodnes of it, which notwithftanding it can not fhew. I denie the antecedent, and confequent.

R.*Some.*

Your eyes are not matches. If they were, you might haue feene very eafily, that no reafon of mine is periured once, much leffe, thrife. I am perfwaded that if you be not well coniured by the Magiftrate, you wil proue a ftrange body. You are farre gone alreadie. Strange fancies haue almoft cõfumed you. The Magiftrates difcipline is the fitteft medicine for you. If that will not recouer you, your difeafe is defperate. You denie both my antecedent, & confequent. My antecedẽt was that vnpreaching Minifters do adde an edifying word to the Element. That there is *verbum ædificans,* I proue it thus. The fumme of Chriftes Sermon in the Inftitution & adminiftration of the holy Supper by himfelfe is the worde of Inftitution in the adminiftration of the holy Supper in the Church of England : therefore, vnleffe we wil denie the fumme of Chriftes Sermon, to bee an edifying worde, (which no learned man will denie) we muft confeffe, that wee haue *verbum ædificans,* that is, an edifying worde, in the adminiftration of the holy Supper with vs.

I.*Penry.*

Your reafon of the antecedent, that the recital of the fumme of Chrifts Sermon, that is, the words of Inftitution, is an edifying worde, is falfe, and

maintaineth

maintaineth charming.For doe you thinke,that the worde of inſtitution, being,as you ſay,the ſumme of Chriſts Sermon,is then an edifying worde, whenſoeuer it is recited by a prophane perſon, euen in the prophanation of Gods ordinance ? Looke 2.*Tim.*4.3. and you ſhall finde that the worde barely read, and to no other purpoſe, then to edifie by reading, is not holſome doctrine. The popiſh prieſt either without or within the booke, pronounceth in his darke Latine,the ſumme of Chriſts ſermon: Is that an edifying word,which he prophanely breatheth ? The word of God vttered,is not an edifying worde,vnleſſe it bee vtered according to the ordinance,both in regard of the perſons that vtter the ſame, and the ende wherefore it is vttered.No learned man wil denie the Lords prayer rightly ſayd,to be an edifying worde. And yet,by your leaue, no learned man, vnleſſe he fauoureth charming or poperie,will ſay that the Lords prayer pronounced by an ignorant man in a ſtrange tongue, or prophaned by a witch,is an edifying word.

R.Some.

M.Penry is now in his Ruffe, His pride and ignorance appeare in their colours. They are proclaimed euen by himſelfe. He denieth that the recitall of the ſumme of Chriſts Sermõ,by an vnpreaching miniſter,is an edifying word : he ſaieth, it maintaineth charming. Can we thinke,that this man is guided by Gods ſpirit,whoſe heart conceiued,and pen broght forth ſuch blaſphemie? That the reader may be aſſured,that the ſumme of Chriſts Sermon,is an edifying word,I will firſt ſet downe the word of Inſtitution, which is the ſumme of Chriſts Sermon, and then proue the point. The word of inſtitution in the holy Supper,is : *The Lord Ieſus the ſame night that he was betrayed,tooke bread: and when he had giuen thanks,he brake it,and ſaide, Take,eate : this is my body, which is broken for you: this doe ye in remembrance of me. After the ſame maner alſo he tooke the cuppe, when he had ſupped,ſaying,this cup is the new Teſtamẽt in my blood:this do as oft as ye drinke it,in remembrance of me. 1.Cor.11.* That this word of Inſtitution doth edifie,it is manifeſt: for it teacheth vs, firſt,who did inſtitute the holy Supper:

ly Supper : *The Lord Iefus.* Secondly, at vvhat time: *The fame night that he was betrayed.*Thirdly,vvhat the Elements are in the holy Supper: *Bread and wine.* Fourthly, what our Sauiour Chriſt did : *Hee gaue thankes,he brake the bread,&c.*Fifthly,what the Lorde Iefus faide when hee deliuered the Elements: *Take, eate,&c.*Doeth this maintaine charming? Is there not edifying in this? If you be not voyde of grace,be aſhamed and ſorie for your blaſphemous levvdnes. An other particuler vvhich you reache vnto vs, is a bird of the fame feather : viz. that the vvorde barely read, and to no other purpoſe then to edifie by rea- ding, is not holfome doctrine. For proofe of this groſſe and blaſphemous errour , you vſe three rea- ſons. The firſt is out of *S. Paul* to *Timothee : The time will come, when they will not ſuffer holfome doctrine : but hauing their eares itching,ſhall after their owne luſtes get them an heape of teachers,* 2.*Tim.4.3.* Therefore the vvord barely read, and to no other purpoſe then to edifie by reading, is no holfome doctrine.This rea- ſon cleaues together like a broken potſheard. I de- nie your argument : The Apoſtle in that Chapter commaundeth *Timothee* to attende carefully vpon preaching,&c. His reaſon is: *Many will loath and hate holfome doctrine: they will chuſe ſuch teachers as wil tickle their eares and feede their humours.* 2. *Tim.4.3.* Such gracelefſe people were in the time of *Eſay* and *Mi- cheas.Eſa.30.Mich.2.* Such were they of *Anathoth* in *Ieremies* time *Ier.11.* Such a one was *Amaziah* of *Ie- roboams* Court in *Amos* time. *Am.7.* Such were in the Churches of *Corinth* and *Galatia* in S.*Pauls* time. Such are they of the fantaſticall crewe in our time, vvhich pike out teachers as rot out of an apple.&c.

Doe

Doe you not perceiue M.*Penry*,howe fitly faint *Paul*
to *Timothee* doeth ferue your turne? you haue bene
verie bold with him. You haue vfed the holy Apoftle as *Cacus* did *Hercules* oxen: therefore I may not
thinke much that my writings are depraued by you.
Your fecond reafon is this: the fumme of Chriftes
fermon,pronounced by a Popifh prieft,either without or within the booke in his darke Latin, is not an
edifying worde: therefore the word barely read,and
to no other purpofe then to edifie by reading,is not
holfome doctrine. Your Antecedent might haue
bene kept in: No man denieth it. It is confeffed by
all of the religion,that the fcriptures deliuered in an
vnknowen tongue doe not edifie. The Apoftle proueth this notably. *1.Cor.14. In linguis quas non intelli-
gimus fardi fumus,Cic.in Tufc.* that is, when vve heare
a ftrange language vve are as deafe men.But I denie
your Argument: it is as ftrange as the Popifh priefts
latine is darke.Euery childe may fee the weakenes of
it.But I muft be content and put it vp.It is fuch ware
as you haue.He that wāteth wood,muft burne turfe.
Your third reafon is: No learned man vnleffe he fauoureth charming or Popery,wil fay that the Lords
prayer pronounced by an ignorant man in a ftrange
tongue, or prophaned by a witche, is an edifying
word: therefore the word barely read & to no other
purpofe then to edifie by reading,is not holfome
doctrine. My anfwere is, I denie your Argument. It
is as weake as a ftaffe of reede.This laft reafon is in
deede the fame with the former. I might tell you if I
lifted, that your caufe is poore and naked,when one
reafon muft be twife periured,&c. *verbum fapienti.*
You know the reft: It came out of your wardroabe.
                    O.   Did

Did any ſtudent euer broche ſuch ſtuffe as this?You
neede not ſtudie for theſe arguments.You may deliuer them *ex tempore*, and powre them out by the do-
ſens. Many Carre-men in London can make better
arguments then theſe. I may ſay to you as *Archida-*
mus ſaid to his ſonne,which was more aduenturous
then became him : *Either adde more ſtrength or be leſſe*
*confident.*You haue heard *M.Penryes* inuincible rea-
ſons.Conſider now theſe wordes of his: No learned
man (ſaith hee) will denie the Lordes prayer rightly
ſaide,to be an edifying worde. I thanke you for this,
and doe conclude thus againſt you : Therefore the
Scripture barely read,and to no other purpoſe then
to edifie by reading, is holſome doctrine : for, the
Lords prayer is a part of the holy Scripture.Thus at
vnwares, he hath ouerthrowen his former fancie. I
ſee now of what force the trueth is.It cannot be hidden long. It will breake out at the laſt, as the Sunne
thorow a blacke cloude. It hath pleaſed *M.Penry* to
deliuer an other ſtrange point of diuinitie in theſe
wordes: viz. The word of God vttered,is not an edifying word,vnleſſe it be vttered according to the ordinance,both in regard of the perſons that vtter the
ſame,& the ende wherefore it is vttered. Is not this
(M Penry) to make the perſon to giue credit to the
holy word of God ? which poſitiõ is very groſſe and
blaſphemous.It is a certaine truth in diuinitie:*Scrip-*
tura eſt, αὐτόπιϛος, that is, the Scripture is of credit in it
ſelfe : it needeth not to borowe credite of any man
whatſoeuer.The reaſon is:*the Scripture is,*θεόπνευϛος,that
is,*inſpired,not of man,but of God. 2.Tim.3.16.2.pet.1.21.*
For the cleare proofe of this point, viz. *that the rea-*
ding of the holy Scriptures doeth edifie, I haue ſet downe
found

founde reasons in the former part of this Treatise.
Thither I referre the godly Reader. *M.Penry* besides
my Antecedent, denied my consequent: viz. that it
is not therefore a Sacrament, becaufe vnpreaching
Ministers do adde an edifying worde vnto the Element. His reason, such as it is, is contained in his
owne words which follow.

I.Penry.

Concerning your consequent, doe you thinke, that euery one, that can
adde an edifying word vnto the Element, may minister a Sacrament? it is
not so: for Paul requireth the wordes of euery Christian (women and all)
to be edifying wordes, *Ephes.4.29*.euen in common talke. Shall therefore
the Element administred by euery Christian, be a Sacrament? God forbid.
And yet euery Christian can adde the summe of Chrifts Sermon vnto the
Element, in the administration of the Supper, which if it were sufficient, as
by your reason it is, then women, children, &c. Idiots that could not reade
might deliuer a Sacrament.

R.Some.

You want matter to vvorke on. That is the caufe,
vvhy you shoote so much at rouers in your Treatife.
If the common speach of euery Christiā must bring
edification and grace, that is, godly profite to the
hearers, *Ephe.4.* What shal we thinke of you, vvhofe
writings haue neither grace nor salt, that is, are neither profitable nor sauory, as the Apostle requireth,
Colof.4. You would beare the vvorld in hand, that, in
my iudgement, euery one vvhich can adde an edifying vvord to the Elemēt, may deliuer a Sacrament:
and so confequently, vvomen, children, idiots. I am
very farre, I thanke God, from this fancie. If you had
any sparke of good nature or common sense in you,
you would not father that on me cōtinually, whereof, not so much as the least print appeareth in my
writings. I perceiue the blacke *More* cannot change
his skinne, nor the *Leopard* his spots. Your absurde
collections

colleƈions are euidences of your ſpirit. They ſhall neuer trouble mee: I will not doe you that pleaſure. *Fruƈtus lædentis in dolore læſi. Tertul. de pat.* that is, the pleaſure which an enemie taketh, is in the griefe of him that is hurt.

R.Some.

If any vvill conclude of this, that I miſlike preaching before the adminiſtration of the Sacrament, he doeth me great wrong.

M.Penry ſaith nothing to this.

An obieƈtion of the fantaſticall ſort.

Vnpreaching Miniſters are not apt to teach : therefore they are no Sacraments which are deliuered by them.

R.Some.

The Argument folowes not.My reaſon is,Many Iewiſh prieſtes were both ignorant and diſſolute in *Eſay* and *Chriſts* time.*Eſay 28,7.Matt.9.36.*But the ſacrifices offred,& the Sacraments reached by them, vvere both Sacrifices and Sacraments. Othervviſe, the Prophetes vvhich vvere at *Ieruſalem,* vvhen the Ievviſh Church vvas full of corruption,vvould not haue bene preſent at,and partakers of the Sacrifices in *Salomons* Temple. *Calu.Inſtit.lib.4.cap.1.ſeƈt.18,19.*

An obieƈtion of the fantaſticall ſort.

Ignorant Miniſters are not apt to teach : therefore no Miniſters, and conſequently,they are no Sacraments which are deliuered by them.

R. Some.

The Argument folovves not.I graunt that it is of the ſubſtance of a lavvful and good Miniſter of God to be apt to teach:but it is not of the eſſence of a Miniſter ſimply : for which it is ſufficient to haue the Churches calling. This appeareth clearely in the Magiſtrate. The holy Ghoſt requireth that none ſhoulde be choſen a Magiſtrate, vnleſſe hee were a

man

man of courage, fearing God, dealing truely, and hating couetoufnes. *Exod.18.21.* When fuch are aduanced as defile their handes, either with filthie bribes, as *Felix* did, or with barbarous crueltie, as *Abimelech* and *Herode* did, fhall we fay that they are no Magiftrates? I confeffe, they are not fingled out by the electors according to Almightie Gods direction in his holy Bible : but they are Magiftrates notwithftanding, and we are commanded by the Lorde to performe all duetie vnto them, *faluo officio*, that is, our duetie being referued to the higheft Magiftrate, which is God himfelfe.

I.Penry.

The reafon concluding vnpreaching minifters to bee none, becaufe they are not apt to teach, you haue twife repeated within one twelue liues, and made two feuerall obiections thereof. That was an ouerfight: the fufficiencie of the argument, I haue fhewed to be fuch, as *Caiphas* miniftery and *Herods* magiftracie brought in by you, will neuer anfwere the fame. Both of them, with the reafon from the outward calling of readers, I referre to your next chapter, where they are repeated: thither nowe I am come, where the contradictory of the queftion fhalbe fet downe and proued briefely: becaufe the nullitie of the vnpreaching miniftery may be in fteade of a thoufand reafons to proue the fame.

R.Some.

My obiections are feuerall, whatfoeuer you fay. Any one that hath but halfe an eye, may eafily fee it by my feuerall anfweres. I haue fet downe the obiections as they were deliuered to me. The confutation of my anfweres, if it be any, is foorth comming, you fay, in an other place. I haue fought for it, but I cannot finde it, It is fhrunke, I feare, in the wetting.

R.Some.

If any fhall gather of this I haue fet downe, that I vndertake the defence of ignorant minifters: my anfwere is, that my writings and Sermons, are not *Aiax* fhielde to couer them, but the Lords fworde to

cutte

cutte them. I confeſſe freely, that I am very farre
from opening either the Church doore to ignorant
miniſters, or the pulpit doore to vnskilfull preachers: which vnskilfull preachers giue Gods religion a greater blowe then the ignorant miniſters: for
in ſtead of diuiding the word of trueth aright, they
ſpeake at all aduentures, yet very boldely: and as vnskilfull Apothecaries, deliuer *quid pro quo*, chaffe for
wheate, and ſtrange fancies for Gods holy trueth.
By ſuch abſurde fellowes, many Churches and excellent men in this land, haue bene greatly diſquie-
ted, and the good courſe of religiõ hath bene greatly hindered. The cauſe of this ſore, is intollerable
pride, and groſſe ignorance in theſe bad companions, and want of care in the Magiſtrates.

I. Penry.

I am as farre from accounting the vnskilfull preachers which ſpeake
hand ouer head they care not what, (againſt whome your complaint is
very iuſt) to be miniſters: as I am from acknowledging many of our abſurde doctors to be apt to teach, who can bring nothing into ẙ Pulpit, but
that which other men haue written: and that very often ſo fit to the purpoſe of edification, as the reaſon from the corner to the ſtaffe is ſoundly
concluded. In theſe three ſortes of ſuppoſed miniſters (and there coulde
be a fourth added vnto them) conſiſteth the woe of our Church.

R. Some.

Is my complaint iuſt againſt vnskilful preachers?
Doe you, *M. Penry*, wipe them out of the rolle of
miniſters? Will you ſhut the pulpit doore againſt
them? Take heede what you doe. You bidde your
ſelfe loſſe. Your kingdome will then fall to the
ground: for vnskilfull preachers are your Bulwarks
and Blockhouſes to ſupport your fancies. The abſurde Doctors you mention, ſhall haue no defence
of mee. If they preach as you write, for that duetie
and loue I owe and beare to the Church and Vniuerſities,

uerfities, I woulde both they & you were difgraded:
and they kept out of the Pulpit, and your writings
out of the Preffe. I hope fome good will growe by
your writings. Firft, that the Vniuerfities will take
better heed, vpon vvhom they beftow their degrees:
Secondly, that the Magiftrates vvill looke better to
the Printing houfes. By the fourth fort of fuppofed
Minifters vvhich you vvrite of, I knovve not vvhom
you meane. I could gheffe fhrevvdly, but I vvil not,
becaufe I vvill not mifconftrue you. If they or any o-
ther be the murraine of our Church, I vvoulde they
vvere either reformed or remooued.

R. Some.

If any fhall aske me what the true caufes are, why
fo many vnfit men are the Churches minifters: I anfwere, either great want of iudgement, or great corruption in fuch, which doe ordeine and preferre
them. The finne of thefe men is very great: for they
difhonour Almightie God, and doe grofly abufe
the people of the land. This difeafe will be healed,
when the Churches maintenance is not difpofed of
by them which haue the golden dropfie, but is freely giuen to worthie and painefull ftudents, which
will neither fifh with the filuer hooke, nor open the
Church doore with a filuer key.

M. Penry fayeth nothing to this.

CHAP.

THE GODLY ARE NOT
polluted which receiue the Sacrament at the hands of an vnpreaching Minister.

I. Penry.

BY pollution I doubt not you meane sinne.

R. Some.

I doe so.

R. Some.

The Sacraments are Gods ordinance: the ministers ignorance can not peruert the nature of Gods ordinance.

I. Penry.

The Ministers ignorance, say you, page 28. cannot peruert Gods ordinance : and againe page 29. the Sacraments are not the worse for the ignorance of the minister,&c. All this I graunt, but bare readers are not ministers, and the doubt is, whether the action performed by them be the ordinance of God, whether it bee a Sacrament. These be the questions which you ought to haue proued, and not haue taken them as principles, though you doe this the third and fourth time.

R. Some.

Your writings are like the winde, not long in one corner. Before you denied it not to be a Sacrament, which was deliuered by vnpreaching ministers: here you doubt of it. You erred either then, or now. Were he not a wise man, that would followe your humour? The rocke he should builde on, should be nothing but sand: his building should be as the wall in *Ezechiel*, dawbed with vntempered morter. If vnpreaching ministers haue administred a Sacrament in your iudgement, I am sure you cannot deny them to haue a calling : for you will not accompt it a Sacrament, which is deliuered by priuate men. But let vs see what you write in an other place of this argument.

I. Penry.

I. Penry.

If vnpreaching minifters be no minifters, and if I cannot be affured to receiue a Sacrament, but onely at the hands of a minifter: then cannot I affure my felfe, that an vnpreaching minifter can deliuer a Sacrament vnto me: and therefore it is vnlawfull for me, or any Chriftian, to goe vnto an vnpreaching minifter for the Sacraments: if vnlawfull, then a finne: if a finne, then the godly are polluted, which goe vnto them for the Sacraments.

R.Some.

If vnpreaching minifters were no minifters (as you affirme and I denie) then I would confeffe that a Sacrament might as eafily be had of them, as water of a drie ditch. But, what if fome did minifter the Sacrament in the Apoftles times, which were not preachers? very famous men are of that iudgement. *Caluine* vpon thefe wordes of the Apoftle, *Chriſt ſent me not to baptize, but to preach the Goſpel, 1.Cor.1.17.* writeth thus: There were fewe to whom the office of preaching was committed: but the adminiftration of Baptifme was committed to many. *Martyr* writeth thus vpon the fame place of the Apoftle: *Munus tingendi, &c.* that is, the adminiftration of Baptifme may bee committed to euery one in the Church, but not the office of preaching. *Chriſoſtome* vpon that place of S. *Paul* hath thefe vvordes: *Euangelizare perpaucorum eſt, &c.* that is, fewe are able to preach, but euery one may baptize, that hath a calling. Of this iudgement are *Ambroſe, Hemingius, &c. Auguſtine* hath thefe wordes: *Perfeĉtè baptizare minùs doĉti poſſunt: perfeĉte euangelizare, multò difficilioris & rarioris eſt operis. Ideo doĉtor gentium, plurimis excellentior, Euangelizare miſſus eſt, non baptizare: quoniam, hoc per multos fieri poterat, illud per paucos, inter quos eminebat. Auguſt.contra lit.Petil.Don.lib.3.cap.56.* I haue not fet downe this as either fword or fhield for

ignorant

ignorant Minifters. My iudgement is, that none ought to enter into,or continue in the holy Minifte-rie,vnleffe they haue giftes in fome meafure. The Plough man may returne to his fhare : the Artificer to his fhop : Other to their feuerall trades. Almigh-tie God will not be offended if they doe thus : Yea, his Maieftie wil be highly pleafed. *Zach.1 3.Ruff.lib.1. cap.6.Melius de media via recurrere, quàm femper curre-re malè.*It is not fafe to continue in a wicked courfe.

R.Some.

A Sacrament can neuer be without promife of faluation: therefore,the worthie partaker of the Sa-cramēt receiues a bleffing : if a bleffing,then no pol-lution. That he receiues a bleffing, the Apoftle tea-cheth vs : *Wee are buried with Chrift* (faith .S.*Paul*) *by baptifme into his death,&c.Rom.6.4. The cuppe of blefsing which wee bleffe, is it not the communion of the blood of Chrift? The bread which we breake, is it not the communi-on of the body of Chrift? 1.Cor.11.16.*

I.Penry.

M.Some faith: the worthy partaker receiues a bleffing : if a bleffing,no pollution,&c.Firft,it is doubted whether we may be affured that it is a Sa-crament.Secondly,he is no worthy receiuer that receiueth of an idole Mi-nifter.Thirdly,there may be a bleffing receiued,& yet pollution in the re-ceiuer.Looke *2.Chro.*30.17.18,19.*Nom.*9.7.

R. Some.

Nodum in fcirpo quæris. You ftumble in the plaine way. My anfwere is : Firft, if the vnpreaching Mini-fter haue a calling, (which no learned man in this land doubteth of)it cannot be denied to be a Sacra-ment. It pleafeth you,*inter facrum & faxum hærere,*to doubt of it.Secondly,whofoeuer bringeth faith and repentance with him to the holy Table, is a worthy receiuer, though the Minifter be an idole. The vn-worthines

worthines of the Minifter hurtes himfelfe, but not
the godly communicant, Otherwife the holy Prophets were vnworthie receiuers, which communicated with idole prieftes. Thirdly, you adde that a
bleffing may be receiued, and yet pollution in the receiuer, *2.Chr.30. Nomb.9.* This is, ἀπροσδέκτευσιν, iuft from
the corner to the ftaffe, that I may vfe your owne
phrafe. Do you confute on this fafhion? You fhould
haue proued that the worthy partaker of the Sacrament receiuing a bleffing, receiued pollution, (that
is finne,) by partaking the Sacrament. Becaufe this
paffeth your skill, you fight with your fhadowe, and
tell me, that a bleffing may be receiued, and yet pollution in the receiuer: That is to fay, that pollution
is brought of the Communicant to the holy table,
not receiued from or by the holy Sacrament. This
makes nothing againft that which I haue written.
Onely it bewrayeth your ignorance. All godly men
confeffe, that pollution, that is finne, is in the holieft
Communicants: I meane, *peccatum habitans non reg-
nans,* That is, finne dwelleth in Gods feruants, but
hath not dominion ouer them. The Patriarks, Naza-
rites, Prophets, Apoftles, had this pollution. They
could not fhake it off in this life: the beft of them had
their wants. Only our Sauiour Chrift was cleare of
finne. You and I agree, I am fure, in this particuler. If
I fhould aske you, how you proue pollution, that is,
finne, to bee in the receiuer of the holy Sacrament,
you woulde referre mee to your quotations in the
booke of *Chronicles* and *Numbers.* Giue me leaue to
examine your quotations a litle. Your firft place is
in the *Chronicles.* The words of the text are thefe: *Becaufe there were many in the Congregation that were not*

sanctified, therefore the Leuites had the charge of the killing of the Paſſeouer, for all that were not cleane, to sanctifie it to the Lord. For a multitude of the people, euen a multitude of Ephraim, and Manaſſeh, Iſſachar and Zebulun, had not cleanſed themſelues, yet did eate the Paſſeouer, but not as it was written : Wherefore Hezekiah prayed for them, saying, The good Lord be mercifull toward him, that prepareth his whole heart to ſeeke the Lord God, the God of his fathers, though hee be not cleanſed, according to the purification of the Sanctuarie. 2.Chr.30.17,18,19. All that you can proue by this place, is, that they of *Ephraim, Manaſ-ſeh, Iſſachar, &c.* were vncleane according to the pu-rification of the Sanctuarie, that is, touching ſome ceremonie of *Moſes* law : for which vncleannes they were diſpenſed with. Your ſeconde place is in the booke of *Numbers.* The wordes of the text are theſe: *And certaine men were defiled by a dead man that they might not keepe the Paſſeouer the ſame day : and they came before Moſes and before Aaron the ſame day. And thoſe men ſaid vnto him, we are defiled by a dead man: wherefore are wee kept backe that wee may not offer an offering vnto the Lord, in the time thereunto appointed, among the chil-dren of Iſrael? Then Moſes ſaid vnto them, ſtand ſtil, and I wil heare what the Lord will cōmande concerning you. And the Lord ſpake vnto Moſes, ſaying, Speake vnto the childrē of Iſrael, & ſay, if any among you, or of your poſteritie, ſhall be vncleane by the reaſon of a corps, or bee in a long iourney, he ſhall keepe the Paſſeouer vnto the Lord. Nu.9.ver.6,7, 8,9,10.* All that you can gather of this place, is, that theſe mē which were defiled by reaſon of a dead mā, did not celebrate the paſſeouer before the Lordes pleaſure vvas knowen. You cannot conclude either of this place in the booke of *Numbers,* or of the for-mer

mer place in the *Chronicles*, that finne was in thefe, which offered themfelues to the Paffeóuer. I doubt not but that thefe men had pollution, that is, finne, in them : But I am fure thefe places neither doe nor can prooue it: for you may not reafon thus : They of *Ephraim* &c. were vncleane touching fome ceremonie of *Mofes* lawe,therefore they were finners. If you do,I deny your argument. It is a certaine truth in diuinitie,that not euery legall pollution was ioyned with finne. My reafon is, the touching of a dead body, was a legall vncleanneffe. If it were a finne, then the buriall of the dead, which is a Chriftian duetie,and a worke of mercy, fhould be finne.Thus, you haue taken paines, but to litle purpofe. You haue fhotte,I confeffe: but, *nec cœlum nec terram attingis,*you are many fcores wide.

R.Some.

The parents of Chrift went to *Ierufalem* euery yere at the feaft of the paffeouer,*Luk.2.41.*Their going to *Ierufalé*, was to teftifie their religion, & to be partakers of the Sacrifices. There were at that time in *Solomons* Temple manifold corruptions: the high priefthood was folde for money,many of the Iewifh prieftes were ignorant, yet *Iofeph* and the virgine *Mary* were not polluted.*Calu. Luc.2.41.*

I.Penry.

The blindneffe of the ignorant Leuites cannot make fuch a nullitie of their priefthood,as they fhould be no priefts vnto the people. And therefore great reafon why the parents of our Sauiour,and the reft of the godly fhould not leaue the feruice of God,for the pollution of the prieftes.

R.Some.

The ignorant Leuites are deepe in your bookes. They find grace with you. You allowe them to be prieftes vnto the Ifraelites, whom Almightie God

neuer approoued : yea, whom his maieftie hath dif-
claymed.*Hof.6.* You muft of force be as beneficiall
to ignorant minifters,vnleffe you doe fimply condemne the externall calling of the minifters in the
Church of *England,*to be none at all. If you doe fo,
then in your iudgement,wee haue no minifterie,no
facraments,no vifible Church in *England.*

R.Some.

The godly which receiue the holy Supper of an
vnpreaching Minifter,are not partakers of the Minifters vnworthineffe, but of the holy Sacrament,
which is a pillar of our faith : therefore the vnworthineffe of the minifter doth not defile the Communicant. *Alterius,fiue Paftoris,fiue priuati indignitate,*
non læditur pia confcientia.&c. Calu.Inftitut.lib.4.cap.1.
*fect.19.*that is,A godly confcience is not hurt by the
vnworthineffe of another,either Paftour or priuate
man:neither are the myfteries leffe pure and healthfull to a holy man, becaufe they are then handled of
fuch as be impure. *Ille qui accipit,fi homo bonus ab ho-*
mine malo,fi fidelis à perfido,fi pius ab impio : perniciofum
erit danti,non accipienti. Illud quippe fanctum malè v-
tentem iudicat,bene accipientem fanctificat. Aug,contra
Cref.gram.lib.2.cap.28. that is,He which receiueth,if
a good of an euill man, if a faithfull of a faithleffe
man,if a godly of a wicked man,it wil bee hurtful to
the giuer,not to the receiuer:for that holy thing(he
meaneth the Sacrament) doth iudge him which v-
feth it ill,but doth fanctifie him which receiueth it
well.

M.Penry anfweres nothing to this.

R.Some.

Circumcifion was one of the Lords Sacraments in
the

the Iewiſh Church, The Iewes which were circumciſed of impure prieſts, and apoſtates, receiued no
hurt : therefore no pollution. *Calu. Inſtitut. lib. 4.
cap. 15. ſect. 16.* The Sacraments neither are, nor can
be the vvorſe for the ignorance or vnworthineſſe, or
better for the learning or worthineſſe of any man
whatſoeuer. Whoſoeuer thinketh otherwiſe, is a
Donatiſt.

I. Penry.

The Sacraments are not the worſe for the ignorance of the miniſter:
All this I graunt &c.

R. Some.

The firſt part of my reaſon is paſſed ouer with ſilence : A breefe kind of anſwering. In this M. *Penry*
reſembles yong children. Where they cannot read
they skippe ouer.

R. Some.

Touching this point of the Sacramẽt, I reſt wholy
in *Auguſtines* iudgemẽt: his words are theſe. *Ego dico,
melius per bonũ miniſtrum quàm per malum diſpenſari Sacramenta diuina : verùm hoc propter ipſum miniſtrum
melius eſt, vt eis rebus quas miniſtrat, vita & moribus cõ-
gruat, non propter illum, qui etiam ſi incurrerit in miniſtrum malum diſpenſantem veritatem, ſecuritatem accipit
à domino ſuo monente ac dicente : Quæ dicunt facite, quæ
autem faciunt, nolite facere : dicunt enim, & non faciunt.
Addo etiam ad hoc eſſe melius, vt ille cui miniſtratur,
miniſtri boni probitatem ac ſanctitatem diligendo faci-
lius imitetur : Sed non ideo veriora & ſanctiora ſunt
quæ miniſtrantur, quia per meliorem miniſtrantur. Illa
namque per ſeipſa vera & ſancta ſunt, propter Deum
verum & ſanctum cuius ſunt, & ideo fieri poteſt vt accedens ad ſocietatem populi Dei, alium inueniat à quo facilè
baptizetur, alium eligat quem ſalubriter imitetur. Certus*

eſt

eſt enim ſanctum eſſe ſacramentum Chriſti,etiamſi per mi-
nus ſanctum,vel non ſanctum hominem miniſtratum eſt,
ſe autem eiuſdem ipſius ſacramenti ſanctitate puniri,ſi in-
dignè acciperit,ſi malè vſus fuerit,ſi ei non conuenienter
& congruè vixerit. Auguſt. contra Creſ. Gram. lib: 4.
Chap.20. The ſumme of *Auguſtines* vvords is, that the
Sacrament is adminiſtred better by a good, then by
a bad miniſter : yet that the Sacraments of themſelues are true and holy,&c. by vvhat miniſter ſoe-
uer they be deliuered,&c. If any ſhall aske me, whether it be lavvfull to omitte the partaking of the holy Sacrament in ſuch Churches, ouer which ignorant miniſters are ſet, and to preſent our ſelues
and our infantes to the holy Sacrament in o-
ther Churches: my anſwere is, that I referre them
to the Magiſtrate and gouernours of our Churches,&c.

Nothing is anſwered to this.

An obiection of a fantaſticall body.

By whom a thing ought not to be deliuered, by another it ought not
to be receiued : but ignorant miniſters ought not to deliuer the Sacraments,therefore &c.

R.Some.

The maior is falſe. My reaſon is. An euill man
ought not to deliuer the word of God, but we ought
to receiue it. An euill man ought not to giue almes,
but a poore man may receiue it. An abſurde miniſter ought not to deliuer the Sacrament, but
they are not polluted which receiue it.

I. Penry.

The obiection concerning the giuer and the receiuer,was neuer mine:
I could turne it againſt you,but I muſt be briefe.

R. Some.

It was not yours,I confeſſe.I doe not charge you
with

with it. It was an other mans. You muſt giue ſome other men leaue to make fond arguments as well as your ſelfe. You could turne it, you ſay, againſt me. You are one of the ſtrangeſt turners that euer I knewe. You haue turned out ſuch a deale of groſſe diuinity vpon me and other, that we are wearie, and you may be aſhamed of it.

CHAP.10.

I.Penry.

THE GODLY DOE SINNE,

which doe communicate with ~vnpreaching~ miniſters.

Reaſons.

Becauſe they communicate with thoſe, who are no Miniſters.

R.Some.

Ou haue bene liberall in charging me to begge the queſtion. It is your fault in this place. You affirme that vnprea-ching Miniſters are no Miniſters : I denie it. It is very ſtrange to mee that you will accompt ignorant Leuitical prieſts lawfull prieſtes, and denie vnpreaching Miniſters to haue any calling. If you were indifferent, you would ſerue them both alike.

I.Penry.

They cannot be aſſured to receiue a ſacrament at their handes.

R.Some.

Your ſelfe denies not that they are the Sacramẽts which are deliuered by vnpreaching Miniſters. If they be the Sacraments which are adminiſtred, I am ſure, firſt, that they are the Sacraments which are re-

Q. ceiued.

ceiued: fecondly, that they haue a calling which do adminifter them. Befides, the ignorance of the Minifter cannot pollute the godly receiuer.

I.Penry.

They do not examine themfelues aright,& fo are not worthy receiuers, 1.Cor.11.28.in as much as they do not acknowledge it a finne to communicate where there is no Minifter.

R. Some.

This reafon is all one with your firſt: therefore it is alreadie anfwered. They which offer themfelues to the holy Table, without due examinatiō of themfelues, are vnworthy receiuers. This examination confifts of faith and repentance.

I. Penry.

Becaufe they either make the element to bee a Sacrament naturally in it felfe, and not by the ordinance of God, or els thinke the ordinance of God in the inftitution of the Sacrament, onely to confift in the recitall of the words: *I baptife thee,&c.* or *take,eate,&c.* whereas a Minifter is a moſt principall part of the ordinance.

R.Some.

You are an vnpleafant Muſician: You harpe ſtill on one ſtring: viz. that vnpreaching Minifters haue no calling. Vnleffe that be graunted, you are at a full point. No godly man that I knowe maketh the element to be a Sacrament naturally in it felfe: or once thinketh that it is a Sacrament, when the wordes of inftitution *I baptize thee,&c.* or *take,eate,&c.* are added to the elemēts, by one that hath no calling. Only *M. Penry* is of that iudgement, which denieth not that they are Sacraments, which are adminiftred by vnpreaching Minifters: and yet thefe Sacraments are but bare elemēts, if vnpreaching Minifters haue no calling, as *M.Pen.* affirmeth. You make the Minifter a moſt principal part of the Sacrament. I graunt the Minifter is an inftrument to deliuer it, but the moſt

moſt principal part & life of the Sacramẽts, depen
deth vpõ Gods promiſes expreſſed in his holy word

I.Penry.

Becauſe they make the Sacraments to be markes no more eſſential vnto the Church,then to other idolatrous Synagogues:for,the element may
be deliuered out of the Church,by a publique perſon,euen as ſubſtãtially,
as by our meere readers.

R. Some.

This reaſon muſt needs be a ſure one,it is ſo hand-
ſomely truſſed together. The godly communicants
confeſſe the Sacraments to be eſſential marks of the
Church, & that idolatrous Synagogues are vnworthie of ſuch precious iewels. I graunt that water,
which is the outward element in Baptiſme, may be
deliuered by any either womã or priuate man without the Church: but, it ſhall not be a Sacrament, as
that is, which is deliuered by vnpreaching Mini-
ſters.If I ſhould tel you,that a Sacrament hath bene
deliuered out of the Church, you would accompt it
a ſtrange paradoxe. What I thinke of it, doeth appeare in an other place of this treatiſe. But, what if
M. Penry denieth not, that baptiſme hath bene and
is deliuered out of the Church? That hee doeth not
deny it,it is manifeſt:His owne words are theſe:Wil
you hold that there is a Church in Popery? the aſſertion is dãgerous,&c.*pag.25*.And a litle after he hath
theſe words : In Popery there is no Church,*pag.27.*
M.Penry in other places of his booke, denieth not
that ſuch as were baptized in Poperie receiued true
baptiſme: therfore he denieth not,that a Sacrament
is deliuered out of the Church,&c. euen by Popiſh
prieſtes which (as hee ſaith)haue no calling at all in
the Church.   *I.Penry.*

They approue the ſinne of the vnpreaching Miniſterie.

R. Some.

The Apoſtles receiued the Lordes Supper with
Iudas : but they did not approue the theft & treaſon
of *Iudas.* The godly which deſire executiõ of iuſtice
at the hands of a heathen or corrupt Magiſtrate, can
not be ſaid to approue either Paganiſme or corruption in the Magiſtrate : for then the Apoſtle ſinned
groſly in appealing vnto *Cæſar, Acts. 25.* The godly
communicants do not approue any ſinne of the ignorant Miniſterie : for they condemne it and pray
againſt it.

I. Penry.

Becauſe they are perſwaded, that Chriſt doeth deliuer vnto them the
ſeales of their ſaluation, by the handes of thoſe that are not Miniſters : to
wit, by vnpreaching readers. In all which points, the godly ſinne, & therefore are polluted in communicating with vnpreaching Miniſters.

R. Some.

Not one learned man in this land that I can heare
of, is ſo perſwaded. They al do confeſſe that vnpreaching Miniſters haue a calling : and that the godly
receiuing the Sacrament at their handes, are partakers of the ſeales of their ſaluation. If you and your
crewe be otherwiſe affected, God ſende you other
mindes.

Iohn Penry. In his addition Page 65.

And I dare arreſt and attaint of high treaſon, againſt the Maieſtie of
the higheſt, all thoſe both men and Angels, who either defende the communicating with them lawful, communicate with them, or tollerate them
as miniſters vnder their gouernement.

R. Some.

You lay on loade : but it is *fulmen ſine tonitru :*
blacke cloudes, but no raine. When your ſingle
arguments will not ſerue the turne, you play the officer, and doe arreſt for traitours againſt God,
all the Magiſtrates and learned men of this lande.
The

The beft is, Almighty God hath not put his mace into your hands. It is a note of a falfe prophet to kill
the foules of them that die not.*Ezech.13.* That they
are not polluted which receiue the Sacraments at
the hands of vnpreaching Minifters, is fufficiently
prooued. Such Bifhops and Patrons, as haue either
ordeined or prefented vnfit men to the holy miniftery and clergie liuings, haue much to anfwere fo-.
I doe not defend or excufe fuch Bifhops, Patrons,
or minifters. I know they haue highly offended the
maieftie of God: and I pray God with all my heart,
that this fore may be healed.

I. Penry.

They of whofe miniftery there is a Nullitie before God, although they
haue an outward calling, ought not to be accompted minifters: therefore
not to be communicated with.

R. Some.

I deny your Antecedent: My reafons are: firft,
there was a nullitie before God of *Caiphas* priefthood: for he entred by money, and the priefthood
was diuided betweene him and *Annas*, againft the
Lords order. *Calu.Luc.3.* yet *Caiphas* is called the
high Prieft by the Euangelifts. *Matth.26. Iohn 18.*
Secondly, there was a nullitie before God, of the
miniftery of fome in *Philippi*, which preached Chrift
of contention, and to adde more affliction to *Paules*
bandes. *Philip.Chap. 1. 15, 16.* But thefe are accompted minifters by the Apoftle *verfe 15.18.* If a-
ny fhall deny, that there was a nullitie before God
of their minifterie, I proue it thus: they had not an
inward calling. M.*Penry* faieth, that an inward calling is contained in the fufficiencie of gifts and wil-
lingneffe to practife them. *Pag.45.* If M.*Penry* meane
the practife of gifts to Gods glory, I fay, Amen, vnto

Q.iij.   it.

it. I confesse that they of *Philippi* had gifts in some measure, but they had not willingnesse to practise those gifts to Gods glory: which willingnesse &c. is one of the necessary branches of an inwarde calling. That they of *Philippi* had not this willingnes &c. it is manifest: for they sought themselues, & practised their gifts wholy to encrease the Apostles afflictions. *I.Penry.*

Concerning the Nullitie of our readers ministery, we are to know, that there is a nullitie of a ministery before God, eyther because the action proceedeth from a corrupt minister, as *Psalm.*50.16. whome God woulde not haue to deale with his ordinances, or from a corrupt and euill ministerie, which is none of Gods ordinance. The action of the former is substantiall in regard of vs : of the latter wee knowe no substance it can haue. Of the former there is a nullitie onely in the sight of God: of the latter, both in respect of the Lorde and also of vs. The nullitie of our readers ministerie is of this latter sort, namely such as we ought in no wise to account a ministery. Whereas therefore you grant that there is a nullitie of our readers ministery before God, and yet affirme them to be ministers, you swarue from the point, and so your answere is nothing to the purpose, but a desiring of the question, after your vsuall manner. As *Caiphas* then, and the rest of the sleepy dogges, against whome the prophet cryeth out, were wicked men, God would not haue such to bee his ministers: hither referre *Esay* 1.13. But as they had the ministery which God allowed of, they were ministers vnto the people. This ministery, our readers want, therefore they can be no ministers, neyther in respect of the Lorde, nor of the Church. *Shemaiah* was a wicked man, and a false prophet, so were the rest of his stampe. The Lord detested both them and their ministerie. *Zephaniah* and *Caiphas* high priests with their company, were as wicked as any of the false prophets, the Lorde abhorred the men, but their ministery was his ordinance. Hence, M *Some,* it followeth, that neither the briberie of your *Caiphas,* nor the blindnesse of your ignorant Leuites, can make such a nullitie of their priesthood, as they should bee no priestes vnto the people. And therefore great reason why the parents of our sauiour, and the rest of the godly wherof you speake, *Page* 28.29. should not leaue the seruice of God for the pollution of the priests. *Esay* speaketh against blind watchmen, *Chap.*56.10. but *chap.*42.19,20. it shall appeare, that they sawe many things, but kept them not. I pray you conferre the places, and it can neuer be prooued, that any of them were so blinde, as they could not declare by preaching the generall vse of the sacrifices and ceremonies. Their wants might be many, but not like the insufficiency of our readers. Be it they were as insufficient, yet their ministerie might be allowable.

R. Some.

Your anſwere conſiſteth of ſeuerall branches. I will handle the chiefeſt of them ſo briefly as I can. Your firſt branch is, that the miniſtery of the ignorant Leuiticall prieſts is allowed of God: but that the outward calling of our vnpreaching miniſters, is not allowed of God. Of this you conclude, that the Leuitical prieſts were miniſters vnto the people (and conſequently that *Ioſeph* and the virgine *Mary* were not polluted by their Sacrifices) but that our vnpreaching miniſters are not ſo to vs. If the action of ignorant miniſters be, as you write, not ſubſtantiall in regard of vs: then you muſt deny (which before you did not) that any Sacrament either was or is deliuered by them. I would fayne know why the miniſtery of the ignorant Leuites ſhould be allowed, and not the miniſterie of ignorant miniſters. I confeſſe freely, that I take their caſes to be like, howſoeuer you mince & ſhift the matter. But I ſmel your meaning: *Latet anguis in herba*, there is a padde in the ſtrawe. To proceede, you ſtand very much vpon the outward calling of the miniſters in our Church. If you repell the vnpreaching miniſter for his ignorance, you can not allowe the ignorant Leuiticall prieſts. If you repell the vnpreaching miniſter, becauſe of his outward calling, you may by the like reaſon diſcharge the worthieſt miniſters in this land of the holy miniſterie: for all haue one and the ſame externall calling in the Church of *England.* If you be ſo affected, the next newes we ſhall heare of you, will be that you ſhake hands with our Anabaptiſticall recuſants. *Vno abſurdo dato, multa conſequuntur.* that is, Euery abſurditie hath many attendantes.

The

The fecond branch of your anfwere, is, a compa-
ring, or rather preferring the ignorant Leuiticall
priefts before our ignorant minifters. *Nobile par*:
neither barrell better herring. I muft a little while
examine this fecond braunch of yours. You tell vs
that the wants of the Leuiticall prieftes might bee
many, but not like the infufficiencie of our readers.
For proofe of this, you quote two textes in the Prophet *Efay*. The firft is contained in thefe wordes:
Their watchmen are all blind : they haue no knowledge:
they are all dumbe dogges : they cannot barke : they lie and
fleepe, and delight in fleeping. Efa. 56. Will you gather
of thefe vvordes, that the ignorant Leuiticall priefts
were more learned and better furnifhed then the
ignorant minifters ? The prophet *Efay* faieth that
thefe Leuitical priefts had neither *rem* nor *fpem*, that
is, that they were woe begone. If you woulde ftudy
feuen yeeres, you could not deuife to fpeake worfe
of the moft ignorant minifters in our Church. The
fecond place of the Prophet hath thefe words : *Who*
is blinde but my feruant ? or deafe as my meffenger that I
fent ? who is blinde as the perfit, and blind as the Lords fer-
uants ? Seeing many thinges but thou keepeft them not ?
opening the eares, but hee heareth not ? Efay 42. Efay
in thefe verfes calleth the Leuiticall priefts blinde
and deafe, not in body, but in heart, becaufe they
did fee and heare Gods iudgements with their bo-
dilie eyes and eares, and did not obferue them
with the eyes and eares of their hearts. You can
not conclude of this place, that the ignorant Leuiticall priefts were deeper clerkes then the ignorant
minifters in the Church of *England*. The thirde
branch of your anfwere is, that the miniftery of *Cai-*
phas

phas was the Lords ordinance. I deny it, and do diſſent from you in this.My reaſon is : *Caiphas* had not
the high prieſthood alone,therefore his high prieſthood was not the Lords ordinance. The Antecedent is manifeſt, for *Annas* and *Caiphas* were high
prieſts together,*Luk.3*. The argument followes : for
the Lords ordinance was that onely one ſhould be
the high prieſt.*Calu* : *Luk.3.2*. You ſay nothing here
of the contentious miniſters of *Philippi*. You take
and leaue at your pleaſure.It pleaſeth you to cal *Caiphas*,my *Caiphas*, and the blinde Leuites,my ignorant Leuites. I ſhould bee ſpedde, I perceiue, if I
would receiue al that you caſt vpon me.Before,you
did lade me with reuerence : now, you throwe *Caiphas* and the ignorant Leuites, as cobble ſtones, at
me.You are very liberall: but I refuſe your gheſts : I
diſclaime them,and returne them to your ſelfe.You
are much fitter to entertaine them, then I : for, you
haue magnified *Caiphas* miniſtery,& are a hot plea-
der for the ignorant Leuiticall prieſts. That appeareth in your wordes which follow.

C H A P. I I.

I.Penry.

VNFITNES TO TEACH,

made not a nullitie of the Leuiticall Prieſts office.

Reaſons.

Becauſe it was ſufficient, to make him a lawfull, though not a good
Prieſt,for him to be of the line of Aaron.

R.Some.

Ou haue examined and cenſured my
reaſons at your pleaſure.I hope,I may
with your good leaue looke a litle vpon yours. My anſwere is : firſt, If your
firſt reaſon be good, then they which
R. receiued

receiued the Sacraments at their handes, were not
polluted. If they were not polluted, what fay you to
thefe arguments? viz. The Sacrament may not be
receiued at his handes, which wanteth outward calling: therefore not at his hands which is deftitute of
the inwarde graces. *I.Pen.* Againe, we haue no warrant to receiue an extraordinarie Sacrament: But
that which is adminiftred by ignorant Minifters is
an extraordinarie Sacrament, if it be any: therefore
we haue no warrant to receiue it.   You know, I am
fure, the father of thefe two arguments. They came
out of your owne Mint. Secondly, if your firft reafon be good, then a corrupt externall approbation
made them lawful Priefts, which had not an inward
calling, that is, fufficiencie of gifts, &c. If you denie
the externall approbation of the ignorant Leuites,
to be a corrupt approbation, I proue it thus. It was a
breach of Gods owne order, therefore it was a corrupt approbation. The antecedét is manifeft in thefe
words: *The Priefts lips fhail keepe knowledge, and they fhall
feeke the Law at his mouth, &c. Mal.2.*Therefore the externall approbation of ignorant Leuites was a corrupt approbation.

I.Penry.

There was no commaundement concerning the triall of his fitneffe to
teache: therefore vnfitneffe to teach made not a nullitie of the Leuiticall
Prieftes office.

R.Some.

You proue your antecedent thus: Almightie God
faid to *Mofes : Thou fhalt appoint Aaron and his fonnes to
execute the Priefts office, &c. Num.3.10.*My anfwere is:
No trial of giftes in *Aaron* & his fonnes was needfull
at the firft: for Almightie God did furnifh thé accordingly. My reafon is côteined in thefe words of God
him-

himfelfe: *My couenant was with him of life and peace, and I gaue him feare, and he feared me, and was afraide before my Name. The Lawe of trueth was in his mouth, and there was no iniquitie found in his lippes : he walked with me in peace and equitie, and did turne many away from iniquitie. Mal. 2.5,6.* God did neuer call any to the holy Mini-ſterie, but he gaue them giftes fit for that function. I haue proued this point in the beginning of this trea-tiſe. To thinke otherwiſe of his Maieſtie, is great wickednes. I hope, you will not reaſon thus : There was no commandement cōcerning the trial of gifts in *Aaron* and his ſonnes at the firſt : therefore there was neuer any triall afterward of giftes in *Aarons* po-ſteritie. If you reaſon thus, I denie your Argument. My reaſon is, If euery one of *Aarons* poſteritie, how vnfit ſo euer, might enter into the Prieſtes office by the Lords warrant, Almightie God might be iuſtly charged to haue had very little care, either of his owne honor, or of the Church of the Iſraelites. Yea, his Maieſtie had flatly broken one of his owne poſi-tiue Lawes conteined in theſe wordes : *The Prieſtes lips ſhall keepe knowledge : they ſhall ſeeke the Lawe at his mouth. Mal. 2.*

I. Penry.

It is not mentioned that any were put from the Prieſthoode for want of this abilitie, whereas the doubt whether they were the ſonnes of *Aaron, Eſ-ra.2.* and their idolatrie, 2. *Chro.* bereaued them thereof : therefore vnſitnes to teach made not a nullitie of the Leuiticall Prieſtes office.

R. Some.

Your reaſon is very weake : It is not mentioned &c. therefore none were. I deny your argument : for it is, *à non ſcripto ad nō factum,* which is not ſure in this caſe. If no ignorant Leuiticall Prieſts were remoued frō the prieſthood, for their vnſitnes to teach : Gods Church

Church had,& the gouernours did, greater wrong.
I am fure, they fhoulde haue bene remoued : for Almightie Gods refolution is flat in thefe wordes : *Be-*
caufe thou haft refufed knowledge, I will alfo refufe thee,
that thou fhalt bee no prieft to mee, &c. Hof.4. The wife
Prince will difplace an abfurde Ambaffadour. The
valiant captaine will remooue a cowardly fouldier.
The husbande man will not fuffer that drudge to at-
tend on his trough,which cannot feede his hogs. If
fuch as were not founde within the compaffe of *Aa-*
rons genealogie,were remoued frõ the Priefthoode,
they had no wrong: for,this was a Law of God himfelfe : *Thou fhalt appoint Aaron and his fonnes to execute*
the priefts office: and, the ftrãger that commeth neere, fhall
be flaine. Numb.3.10. If fuch as committed idolatrie,
were difcharged of the Priefthood, they were iuftly
dealt with. *Ezech.44.*

I. Penry.

The example of *Paul, Acts.*21.26 confirmeth this,who communicated
fince his conuerfion with thofe priefts that were as vnlearned as euer any:
which hee would not haue done, if inabilitie to teache, had made them no
priefts.   Now therefore *M.Some,*to make your Argument from the Leuitical priefthood to be forcible for your vnpreaching Minifters,you muft
prooue, that either our Readers Minifterie is a Leuiticall Minifterie, that
the continuance thereof is vnder the new Couenant,or fhew that the corrupt approbation, (for fo I name the beft outwarde calling they can haue
of the Church)is as forcible to make them Minifters,as was the ordinance
of God to make the fonnes of Aaron facrificing at *Ierufalem,* to be priefts.

R. Some.

How learned or vnlearned the priefts at that time
were in *Ierufalem,*appeareth not in that place of the
Actes. The meaning of *S. Luke* is this : The Apoftle
Paul was accompted by the Iewes an enemie of *Mo-*
fes Lawe. To cleare himfelfe of this,hee entred into
Salomons Temple by the aduife of the Apoftle *Iames,*
and of the brethren in *Ierufalem,* and was purified.
Acts.

Acts.21.26. Your laſt reaſon ſerues very fitly for my
purpoſe : therefore I will vſe it as a ſworde to cut in
pieces ſome of your fancies. *Paul,* you ſay, communicated after his conuerſion with thoſe prieſts, that
were as vnlearned as euer any, & was not polluted.
Of this I conclude:therefore they which receiue the
Sacraments at the hands of vnpreaching Miniſters,
are not polluted.My reaſon is:The ignorant Leuites
and ignorant Miniſters agree *in eodem tertio,* that is,
in ignorance. But *M.Penry* replies that an argument
from the Leuiticall prieſthoode, is not forcible for
vnpreaching Miniſters. To proue this,he vſeth two
reaſons. The firſt is : our readers Miniſterie is not a
Leuiticall Miniſterie, therefore an Argument from
the Leuitical Prieſthood,is not forcible for vnpreaching Miniſters.My anſwere is: I graunt that no miniſterie in theſe dayes is a Leuiticall miniſterie : for,
the date of that miniſterie is out long ago. But I denie your Argument. My reaſon is: An argument is
and may be forcibly drawen from one thing to another, which are vnmatchable. All Logicians confeſſe that ſimilitudes are of things which differ.Eue-
ry meane Sophiſter in the Vniuerſitie knoweth it. It
is very like that you haue forgottē it. Such trifles are
too baſe for your great ſpirits. Your ſecond reaſon
is : The corrupt approbation of vnpreaching Mini-
ſters(ſo you name the beſt outward calling they can
haue of the Church)is not ſo forcible to make them
Miniſters,as was the ordinance of God to make the
ſonnes of *Aaron* ſacrificing at *Ieruſalē,* to be prieſtes:
therefore an Argument from the Leuiticall prieſthood is not forcible for vnpreaching Miniſters. My
anſwer is: I deny your antecedent,and do adde this:

firſt, that it is as lawfull (that is to ſay, vtterly vnlawfull) to make vnfit Miniſters now, as it was before to
make vnfit prieſtes. Secondly, that it was not Gods
pleaſure, that all the poſteritie of *Aaron* without exception, that is, tagge and ragge, ſhoulde be admitted to the holy prieſthood. For neither you, nor any
man aliue, may reaſon thus : The Leuiticall prieſthoode muſt reſt in the tribe of *Leui* : therefore euery
one of that tribe (though vnfit for that holy functiõ)
was to be admitted to the prieſthoode. You might
very ſoundly haue diſputed thus : The Leuiticall
prieſthood muſt be kept within the compaſſe of the
tribe of *Leui*, by Gods expreſſe commaundement,
Num.3. therefore no ſtranger might come neere the
Lords altar. You call the beſt outward calling in the
Church of *England*, a corrupt approbation. If you
meane it is corrupt in admitting ignorant men to
the holy Miniſterie, ſo was the ordeyning of ignorãt
Leuites at *Ieruſalem*. If you meane that the beſt outward calling in the Church of *Englãd*, is ſimply corrupt, that is, none at al, though ſufficient men be admitted, I deteſt your Anabaptiſtical fancie : for then
the worthieſt Diuines in this land, are no Miniſters.
Beſides, it is confeſſed of all famous & learned men,
that Gods Church is not neceſſarily tied in all places and times, to one forme in the externall calling
of the miniſters.

CHAP.

I. Penry.

THE CORRVPT ALLOW-
ance of the *Church* cannot make *our readers*
to be *substantiall Ministers.*

⌐r to all men & women without or within the Church, might be capable of the Ministerie, becaufe all may be capable of this outward allowance. Secondly and particularly, a man not furnifhed with naturall capacitie: thirdly, a man that could not reade, though he wanted alfo the gift of interpretation : for, fuch a one might recite the liturgie without the booke: fourthly ỹ Church might make a man Minifter againft his will, though he fhould neuer confent thereunto. And this is the willingnes that I meane, when I fay, that the inward calling is conteined in the fufficiencie of giftes, and willingnes to practife: which willingnes, I gather vpon the wordes, ὲπιθυμῖι, and ὀρίγεται, vfed of the Apoftle, 1. *Tim.* 3.1. Your reafon therefore from the malicious Philippian Minifters, toucheth not the queftion. Thus *Caiphas* with his crew of vnworthy and monftrous prieftes (who within a few pages, in your booke haue impudently fo often troubled the Reader) is anfwered. And I thinke it a great iudgement of God, that the ornaments of our Englifh and Welch Miniftery, for the moft part, confifteth in the deformitie of fuch lothfome fpots.

R.Some.

If by fubftantial Minifters, you meane fuch as are furnifhed with giftes in good meafure, it is the peculiar office of God to make fuch, either miraculoufly, as hee did the Prophets and many in the Primitiue Church : or by bleffing mens godly ftudies, as in later and our times. It paffeth the Churches reach, by any externall calling to make men furnifhed minifters, which before the external allowance, were not furnifhed by God himfelfe : therefore to bee of the line of *Aaron*, did make the ignorant *Leuites* no more to be fubftantiall prieftes, then the externall calling nowe, doeth make ignorant men to be fubftantiall Minifters. The fumme of your reafons may be fhut

vp

vp briefly in this argument: All may be capable, as
you fay, of the outward allowance: therefore the outward calling of the Church makes not a Minifter to
vs, vnleffe he haue the inward. Your antecedent is a
fpeciall one. If you were not ftrangely caried, fome
branches of it might haue bene kept in. I truft you
do not condemne a prefcript liturgie in the Church
of God. If you do, all the reformed Churches diffent
from you, and their practife doeth apparantly confute you. But I leaue that, and denie your argument.
My reafons are: firft, the ignorant *Leuites* had an outward calling, but not an inward: yet they were lawful priefts by your owne confeffion. Secondly, *Iudas*
was called outwardly, but not inwardly: yet he was
an Apoftle. Laftly, the Apoftle chargeth *Timothee*
not to lay handes rafhly on any, *1.Tim.5.* therefore
the outwarde allowance is more then you accompt
of. My reafon from the côtentious Minifters of *Philippi, &c.* was a very fure one, & did ouerthrow your
fancie. Becaufe you cannot anfwere it, you tell me, it
toucheth not the queftion. A briefe kinde of anfwering. *Caiphas* and the Leuiticall priefts haue bene alledged no otherwife by mee, then by thofe worthy
men *Caluine, Beza, &c.* before mee. The mention of
them hath not troubled the godly Reader at al, therefore not impudently, as you giue out very fawcily. I
perceiue they haue diftempered you: for in fteade of
anfwering my argument, you exclaime vpon them.
Your gift in anfwering, is very rare. You make wafh-
way of the weightieft argumêts. Vnto the lothfome
fpots in the *Englifh* and *Welch* Miniftery, God graunt
either fouèraigne medicine to cure them, or founde
expulfion to remoue them.

R. Some.

R. Some.

Laftly, if your antecedent be true, viz. that they of whofe minifterie there is a nullitie before God, although they haue an outward calling, ought not to be accōpted minifters : what fay you to this propofition ? They of whofe magiftracie there is a nullitie before God, though they haue an outward calling, ought not to be accompted magiftrates. Doe you not thinke this propofition to bee very dangerous ? I could preffe and follow this very farre, but I abftaine of purpofe.

I. Penry.

You demaund what I thinke of this propofition. Surely my iudgement is, that it is altogether without fenfe, and ouerthroweth it felfe : for, it is as if you fayd, he of whofe faith there is a nullitie before God, though he be affured of his faluation, is not to be accompted a faithfull man. Why ? to be affured of faluation, and to haue a nullitie of faith before God, can not ftand together. No more can the outward calling of the magiftracy, ftand with the nullitie thereof. For the outward calling maketh a fubftantiall magiftrate. But, M. *Some,* where is that reafon which you could preffe fo farre ? is this it ? they of whofe magiftracy there is a nullity before God, ought not to be accompted magiftrates. I fay, your propofition is true: affume what you will, you know what maner of nullitie I meane.

R. Some.

My propofition in your iudgement is without fenfe. You are very peremptory. A word, I perceiue, and a blowe. I may fay truely that your anfwere is without fenfe. I grant, that the outward calling maketh a wicked man a fubftantiall magiftrate in that towne or Citie, ouer which he is fet : But I am very fure, that becaufe he wāteth the inward calling, &c. that almightie God doth not allow that magiftrate. My proofe is contained in thefe words of God himfelfe : *They haue fet vp a king, but not by mee : they haue made Princes, and I knewe it not. Hof. 8.* that is, I did not confent vnto it and allow it. The reafon is: Almigh-

S. tie

tie God had appointed the pofteritie of *Dauid* to fit
in the feat of that kingdome, vntil the comming of
chrift. The Ifraelites did fet vp *Ieroboā* &c. It pleafed
you to write, that they of whofe minifterie there is a
nullitie before God, that is, that they whō God hath
not furnifhed with gifts, are not to bee accompted
minifters of vs. I doe fee no reafon, why in your
iudgement, (I fay yours, not mine) there fhould not
be the like fenfe of this propofitiō, viz. they of whofe
magiftracy there is a nullitie before God, that is,
that they whome the Lord hath not furnifhed with
giftes &c. are not to bee accompted magiftrates
of vs. I grant, that both miniftery and magiftracie
are Gods ordinance: but euery minifter and magiftrate is not fo. If they were, wee coulde not diftin-
guifh as we may betweene *rem & perfonam*, that is,
betweene the man and the function.

CHAP. 13.

I.Penry.

THERE BE THREE ESSEN-
*tiall differences betweene an euill magiftrate
and a reading minifter.*

1.

He outward calling of an euill Magiftrate, maketh him
a fubftantiall Magiftrate: fo cannot the outward alow-
ance of Readers, make them to be Minifters.

R.Some.

I graunt, that there are and may be
many more effentiall differences betwene Magiftrates & Minifters, then you fet downe.
Yet this *fimile* fhall be good for matter and maner in
this fort: viz. Vnfit Magiftrates outwardly called are
Magiftrates

Magiſtrates to vs, therfore vnfit Miniſters outwardly called are Miniſters to vs. My reaſon is: the aboue
named Magiſtrates and Miniſters agree in vnfitnes
and outwarde allowance. I confeſſe, that vnfit men
ought not to be aduanced, either to Magiſtracie or
Miniſterie: yet the actiōs of vnfit both Miniſters and
Magiſtrates, are ſubſtantiall to vs, vntill they be remoued. That an argument may very fitly be drawen
from the magiſtracie to the miniſterie, appeareth by
this litle which I haue deliuered. To proceede, I doe
not ſee, why the outward allowance of the Church,
doeth not diſtinguiſh vnpreaching Miniſters from
priuate men, as well as outwarde baptiſme doeth diſtinguiſh ſuch as are baptized, from Paganes.

I. Penry.

2   The Magiſtracie of an euill Magiſtrate, may be allowable before
God: ſo cannot the Miniſterie of Readers.

R. Some.

In your ſeconde difference, the Magiſtracie and
Miniſterie are ſtrangely ſorted. You ſhould haue ſet
it downe thus: the Magiſtracie of an euil Magiſtrate
may be allowable before God, ſo cannot the miniſterie of euill Miniſters. If you had matched them ſo,
I woulde haue anſwered, that both Magiſtracie and
Miniſterie is of God, whatſoeuer the Magiſtrate or
Miniſter is. If you will not deliuer your ſecond difference otherwiſe then you haue, I anſwere firſt, that
the Magiſtracie of *Pilate, Licinius, &c.* was of God,
though his Maieſtie deteſted ſuch Magiſtrates: Secondly, that though ignorant men are not allovved
by Almighty God for good and ſufficient miniſters,
yet the outvvarde calling doeth diſtinguiſh them to
vs, from priuate men: othervviſe it vvere vvide vvith
your ignorant *Leuites.*

3. Men may be affured,to receiue that according to the ordinance of God fubftantially, at the handes of an euill Magiftrate,which concerneth them to haue from him:fo can they not of a bare Reader : for there is no man that can affure himfelfe to be partaker of a fubftantiall Sacrament,at the handes of fuch : and preach they cannot. I haue handled this point of the Magiftracie in my former booke,from page 47.to 51.

R.*Some.*

There is fome good thing, I côfeffe, in the vvorft gouernment: therefore the Philofophers refolution is, that it is better to liue vnder a tyrant, then vnder no gouernour. In this laft difference of yours, you giue me fome aduãtage: for the corrupt Magiftrate hath and may peruert iuftice, that is, fell the righteous for filuer and the poore for fhooes : but the ignorant minifter cannot peruert the Sacramêt which is Gods ordinance: and you haue giuen out often in your Treatife,that you denie them not to be the Sacraments of Baptifme and the holy Supper, vvhich are deliuered by vnpreaching Minifters. You confeffe in this place, that Magiftracie is the ordinance of God. You fay very truely : but, in your *Addition* whither you referre me,you haue hãdled that point vvith very foule and bepitched handes. In your *Addition* you vfe thefe vvords, viz. Magiftracie is an humaine ordinance,that is,as you expounde it,not an Ecclefiafticall conftitution prefcribed in the word. This is a very groffe and Anabaptifticall errour. Almightie God faith thus : *By mee Kings reigne. Prou.8.* Our Sauiour *Chrift* a litle before his condemnation, anfvvereth *Pilate* which was gouernour of *Iudea* vnder the *Romanes*,in this fort:*Thou couldeft haue no power at all againft mee, except it were giuen thee from aboue.* *Iohn.19.* The Apoftle *Paul* writeth thus : *There is no power but of God : and the powers that bee, are ordeined of*

God:

God : whofoeuer therefore refifteth the power , re-fifteth the ordinance of God Rom.13. The Greeke Poet can teach you this Leffon: τιμη,ἐκ Διος ἐςι. Euery learned man knoweth , firft, that the ciuill gouernement before,in,and after the time of *Nimrod,* and after the departure of the Ifraelites out of *Egypt,* vntill their entrance into the land of *Chanaan ,* and in *Chanaan* vntill and after the captiuity in *Babylon,*was the Lords ordinance,& appeareth in Gods booke. Secondly, that the difpofing of the foure famous *Monarchies,*viz. the firft of the *Chaldeans,*the fecond of the *Medes* and *Perfians,* the third of the *Macedonians,* the fourth of the *Romanes,*was Gods ordinance, and fet downe in his holy booke. Laftly, the reuerēce of the Magiftrates which is printed by almightie God in the hearts of fubiects & inferiours , doth cry aloude againft you,that magiftracy is not a deuife of man,but an Ecclefiafticall conftitution and ordinance of almighty God, prefcribed in his holy worde. If you tell me, that the Apoftle *Peter* calleth magiftracie an humaine ordinance, *1.Pet.2:* I grant he doth fo : but his meaning is not, that magiftracy was ordeined and deuifed by man, but by almighty God,for the benefit of man. No man,vnleffe he bee an Anabaptift,expounds the Apoftle *Peters* words as you doe:fo that,not the Apoftles wordes,but the fenfe which you giue them, is Anabaptifticall. *Non fcriptura,fed fenfus fcriptura,eft hærefis.* that is,Not the fcripture,but the fenfe of the fcripture,is herefie.

S.iij.   CHAP.

I. Penry.

WHETHER THE GODLY
doe finne, which receiue the holy Sacrament
at the hands of an vnpreaching Minifter.

He Sacrament may not be receiued at his handes, which wanteth outward calling: therefore not at his hands, who is deftitute of the inward graces.

R. Some.

Your Antecedent is true, and maketh againft the Anabaptifts. I deny your argument. My reafon is : *Omnia Sacramenta cum obfint indignè tractantibus, profunt tamen per eos dignè fumentibus. Aug. contra epift. Parmen. lib. 2. ca 10.* that is, all Sacraments, though they hurt fuch as doe handle them vnworthily, yet they profit fuch, as doe worthily receiue them at their handes.

I. Penry.

My reafon concluding the vnlawfulneffe of communicating with readers, hauing but an outward calling, becaufe it is a finne to communicate with them, which only want the fame hauing fitneffe to teach, is fuch, as I cannot but maruaile, that you would thinke it could be anfwered by a defiring of the queftion, which is a fault in reafoning, wherein belike you feeme to take delight. You fay againe, that readers deliuer a Sacrament. How can we be fure thereof? and why may not I fay as well, that a man indued with gifts to teach, doth deliuer a Sacrament, though he haue no outward calling ? which affertion would be falfe.

R. Some.

You are the ftrangeft anfwerer that euer I met with. I muft be content & anfwere you. If they finne which receiue the Sacraments of him which hath an outward calling and wants the inward : then many godly Ifraelites were polluted which receiued the Sacraments of the ignorant Leuiticall prieftes, which had an outward but not the inward calling.

You

You denie the latter, therefore you cannot affirme the former, vnleſſe you be voyde of common ſenſe. *Petitio principij*, begging of the queſtion is a ſpeciall pearle in your booke. You charge me to delight in it. I vſe it not: there is neither pleaſure nor profit in it. You are a priuiledged man: you may ſay what you liſt. The beſt is, I can receiue no diſgrace by any ſpeeches of ſuch as you are.

I. Penry.

We haue no warrant to reeiue an extraordinarie Sacrament: But that, which is adminiſtred by ignorant miniſters, is an extraordinary Sacrament if it be any: Therefore, we haue no warrant to receiue it.

R. Some.

I deny your Minor, and doe adde this: firſt, that it is a Sacrament by your own confeſſion, *pag. 50. 51.* which is adminiſtred by ignorant miniſters. Secondly, that it is no extraordinarie Sacrament, which is deliuered by them, vnleſſe you will call Baptiſme and the holy Supper, extraordinarie Sacraments.

I. Penry.

By an extraordinary Sacrament, I meane Baptiſme or the Lords Supper, adminiſtred eyther priuately by a miniſter, or any way by one that is no miniſter. I neuer affirmed, the Elements deliuered by readers to bee Sacraments. It is one thing not to deny them, an other thing to affirme them to be Sacraments: The former I haue written, the latter I neuer did: and they doe my writings great iniurie, that report the contrary.

R. Some.

In the ſhutting vp of your Treatiſe, you haue broched two errours, the one is, that it is an extraordinarie Sacrament, which is deliuered any way by one that is no miniſter. Of this I gather, that you holde, that one which is no miniſter, may deliuer a Sacrament: for, an extraordinarie Sacrament is a Sacramēt. If I would enter into your vaine, I might ſet downe theſe conſequents : viz. that bargemen,

children,

children, women, Idiots &c. in your iudgement, may adminifter an extraordinary Sacrament. Your other errour is,that the holy Supper &c. is an extraordinary Sacrament, when it is deliuered priuately by a minifter. I am not of your iudgement in this : I am of M. *Caluines*: therefore I fet downe this propofition : viz. that it is lawfull to adminifter the holy Supper in a particuler houfe, if fome cautions and circumftances be obferued. The reafons do appeare a litle after. It pleafeth you to fay, that as you neuer denied,fo you neuer affirmed it to be a Sacrament,which is deliuered by an vnpreaching minifter. A worthy refolution. If you denie not that it is a Sacrament, &c.you doe affirme it. For, not to deny is to affirme. Euery child can teach you that leffon. I doe leffe meruaile that you are fo fhort and wide in excellent pointes of diuinitie, when you faile in a common point of Grammer. Thus, I fee how complete a man you are.

R. Seme.

If any will conclude of thefe my anfweres, that I miflike M.*Penries* defire of a learned minifterie in *Wales*, hee takes vp that, which I neuer let fall: for I defire with al my heart,and the Lord for his Chrifts fake grant it,that not onely *Wales* may be furnifhed with worthy gouernours and paftours,but all other parts of her Maiefties Dominions, that Gods graces may be more and more multiplied vpon vs and our pofteritie,and his holy hand watch ouer vs.

M.*Penry* fayeth nothing to this.

Chap.

R.Some.

IT IS LAWFVL TO ADMI-
niſter the holy Supper in a priuate houſe, if
ſome cautions be obſerued.

The cautions which muſt be obſerued,are:
Calu.Epiſt.363.
1. *That there be a conuenient nomber to communicate with the ſicke partie.*
2. *That the holy Supper bee deliuered according to
Chriſtes Inſtitution.*
3. *That the explication of the myſterie bee ioyned
with the action.*

M.Caluines reaſons.*Epiſt.363.*

T is forcible for the confirmation of faith, to receiue a pledge, as it were,of Chriſtes hand, whereby wee may bee more aſſured,that wee are of his body, and that we are fed with Chriſtes fleſh and blood,vnto hope of eternall life.

The receiuing of the holy Supper, doeth arme vs in our ſpirituall batraile : therefore the godly ſicke man,is not to be barred of that ſinguler comfort.*An eripiendum eſt ſingulare adiumētum,quo fretus ad luctam alacriùs deſcendat, & victoriam obtineat?*

The holy Supper is a ſigne of holy vnitie amongſt Gods children : therefore the godly ſicke man,whether hee haue a languiſhing ſicknes, or be at deathes doore, is not to be barred from profeſſing his vnitie and conſent with Gods Church.

Cæna,ſancta inter filios Dei vnitatis eſt Symbolum.

If any ſhall reply that the holy Supper, is not a priuate action of any houſholde, but meere Eccle-

T   ſiaſticall:

fiafticall: *1.Cor.11.* M. *Caluines* anfwere is, that the holy Supper deliuered to a godly ficke man, is part of the publique action. *Partem vel appendicem effe conftat publicæ actionis.* M. *Caluine* addeth thefe words:

Neque verò Paulus,dum Corinthios admonet,domum cuique fuam effe in qua comedat & bibat, Cœnam excludit à priuatis ædibus. Tunc neque fidelibus patebant templa, neque vnquam permiſsum eſset noua extruere. Sed tantùm à communibus epulis difcernit ſpirituale myſterium, ne cum illis mifceatur. That is, *Paul* when he doeth admonifh the *Corinthians* that they haue priuate houfes to eate and drinke in, doeth not fhut the holy Supper from priuate houfes: For then, the faithful neither had vfe of any Churches, nor were fuffred to build new. Only he diftinguifheth the fpirituall myfterie frō common banquets, left it fhould be mingled with them.

The fame M.*Caluine* a litle after, hath thefe words: *Cæterum diligenter cauendum eſse fateor, ne qua obrepat fuperftitio, ne ſpes falutis externo Symbolo affigatur, &c.* That is, diligent care muft be had, that no fuperftition creepe in, and that no hope of faluation be tied to the externall figne, &c.*Epiſt.363.*

Of this iudgement is *Peter Martyr* in his Commentarie vpon the *10.chap.ad Cor.Fol.143.*

Chemnicius writeth that it is an abfurde thing to tie the holy Supper to peculiar places : *Ad fubftantiam Sacramenti, ficut non pertinet circumftantia temporis, ita nec circumftantia loci, tanquā neceſaria requiritur. Chemn. in 2.parte exam.con. Trid.* That is, as the circumftance of the time, is not neceffarily required to the fubftance of a Sacrament, fo neither the circumftance of place.

I reft in the iudgement of thefe excellent men. If
                                                   you

you diſſent from mee, I pray you condemne theſe learned writers : but, not before you haue confuted their reaſons.

CHAP. 16.

I.Penry.

Hus *M. Some*, I haue runne therowe thoſe pointes in your booke that concerned me. I haue bene driuen to deale brieflyer therin, then I had determined. But I am enforced to ende,& to omit that, which page 9. I promiſed to handle in the latter ende, with diuers other things. I haue not the like libertie for Printing that you, M.*Some*, doe enioy. Procure me but the fauour to be iudicially heard according to the word, and I will perſonally vpon the perill of my life, by the Lords aſſiſtance, defend theſe two points againſt all gaineſayers. I am ſory, that you whom I reuerence, ſhould be the inſtrument to oppugne a trueth. The Lorde reſpect the cauſe of his owne glory, and pardon our ſinne. Amen.

R.Some.

You haue runne your ſelfe out of breath. You had dealt more wiſely, if you had gone with leſſe haſte and better ſpeede. *Sat citò, ſi ſat bene.* The breuitie which you giue out you are driuen to, is, *dignum patella operculum*, a fit garment to couer your abſurde writings. You haue not, you ſay, ſuch libertie of printing, as I. No reaſon you ſhould. You broche and print groſſe errours and Anabaptiſtical fancies : ſo do not I. You refuſe to offer & ſubmit your writings to the view and allowance of the Magiſtrates : ſo do not I. You would haue me procure you Iudicial hearing,&c. Your requeſt is not equall. *Nec te noui, nec vbi ſis.* Speake for your ſelfe in Gods Name: ſo will I, if you will reuoke your errours and hereſies. Otherwiſe, I will not open my lippe for you, or any ſuch as you are. After leaue obteined, you will appeare (you ſay) though it coſt you your life, and deale in Argu-

T.ij.   ment,

ment, &c. Oh noble *Goliath!* Doe you challenge all gainefayers? fo did the *Donatifts* in *Auguftines* time. *Aug.contra Don.poft Coll.* fo did *Photinus* a groffe heretike in *Bafils* time. *Sozom. lib.4. cap. 6.* fo did Popifh *Campian* in our time. Alas, good *M.Penry*, you are vtterly vnfit for fuch a match. This heate of yours, is like a blaze of thornes. It will laft but a while. Your caufe is naught: your armour is not of proofe. Your Diuinitie is at a low ebbe. Your Arguments are pitifull: your anfweres are filly. There is no hope of preuailing. The *Donatifts, Photinus* and *Campian* prefumed of a glorious victorie: but they were learnedly confuted. The *Donatifts* by *Auguftine: Photinus* by *Bafill* of *Ancyra:Campian* by fome of our learned men. Befides, their garland was *pœna perfidiæ, non corona fidei.* I would be fory, your garland fhoulde be of fuch floures. The beft conqueft that you can haue, is, to ouercome your pride by humilitie, and your ignorance by godly ftudie. Βροτοῖς, ἀ δεύτεραι φροντίδες, σοφωτεραι.*Eurip. in Hippol.* Excellēt men haue their fecond thoughts, wifer then their firft. *Non vincimur, quum meliora nobis offerūtur, fed inftruimur. Cipr.ad Qu.fratrem.* It is no difgrace to yeeld to better things. You are fory, that I, whom you reuerence, fhould be an inftrument to oppugne a trueth. Be fory for your felfe. Deteft your fancies. Your reuerēce I make very meane accompt of. You are the firft that euer charged me in writing to oppugne Gods trueth. I am very farre, I thanke God, from that great finne. Gods trueth, I truft, is as deare to me as to you. I hope it hath had, and fhall haue more defence by me, then by you: there is fome reafon it fhould. You mifliked my laft Treatife: if this booke finde the like grace at your hands, I muft and

will

will beare it. To your prayer, that the Lord would respect the caule of his owne glory, and pardon our sinnes, I say withall my heart, Amen. I haue now, thanks be to God, passed thorow your booke. I haue not runne, but walked a foote pace thorowe it. Your abſurdities, I confeſſe, are brambles, but they haue not pricked me. I would some others tooke no more hurt by them. If my Treatise shall doe either you, or any of your followers good, I will be glad: If not, I say with the holy Apoſtle, *If any man be ignorant, let him be ignorant.*
1.Cor.14.38.

Non habet Dei charitatem, qui Ecclefia non diligit vnitatem. Aug. de baptiſ. contra Don. lib. 3. cap. 16.

T.iij.

T hath pleafed *M. Penry* to take fome paines in prouing that Popifh Prieftes are no lawfull and good minifters of God, that is, that they haue no lawfull calling. In this hee fighteth with his fhadow: for he hath not any of the religion his aduerfarie. I miflike the Popifh priefthoode and facrifice, as much as he: and if occafion require, vvill fet dovvne fure reafons to fhake them both in pieces. That vvhich I holde in this controuerfie, is, that Popifh prieftes haue a calling though a faultie one. If *M.Penry* wil improue that, he muft take penne in hand and begin a frefh : for, as yet he hath not encountred with that particuler. If he can preuaile in that, the famous writings of *Caluine, Beza, &c.* and the refolution of all the *reformed Churches*, in which I reft for this point, fhal be condemned, and *M.Penry* fhall haue the garland. Becaufe I purpofe to paffe, fo briefly as I can, thorow his Treatife of the Popifh priefts, I will handle firft certaine propofitions which are incident to that difcourfe.

The Popifh Church is a Church though not a found Church.

1. The Pope is *Antichrift*, therefore the Church of *Rome* is a Church.

No Proteftant doubteth of the antecedent, &c. I proue my argument thus : *Antichrift fhall fit in the*

Temple

Temple of God. 2.Theſ.2.4. Per Templum Dei, Eccleſiæ perſeſionem,regnum intelligitur.Muſc.2.Theſ.2.4. that is, by the Temple of God, the Church : by ſitting, a kingdome is vnderſtanded.

Viretus a man of excellent learning, writeth thus of the popiſh Church: *Non dum eò vſ̃q̃ degenerauit, & prolapſa eſt, vt eadem prorſus à nobis iudicari debeat, & eo haberi in loco,quo aut Mahumetana,aut Iudaica,quæ Chri-ſtum penitus repudiant, & ab eius legibus & inſtitutis ab-horrent.Nam,ſi nulla omnino extarent in ea,veteris Eccle-ſiæ veſtigia, Daniel non prædixiſſet,futuram abominatio-nem in loco ſancto,neque Paulus, perditum illum filium,in Templo Dei ſeſſurum. Quomodo enim ſederet Antichri-ſtus in Templo Dei,ſi nulla amplius ſupereſſent illius Tem-pli ſaltem reliquiæ,& aliqua ruinarum veſtigia? aut, quo-modo occupare abominatio locũ ſanctum, ſi totus adeò eſſet profanatus,vt ne vllus quidem vel exiguus angulus priſti-næ ſanctitati relictus eſſet? Nam,etſi præualet,ac latius do-minari videtur, hominum iudicio, impietatis regnum: Et Chriſti Eccleſia vſqué eò oppreſſa, ac pene ſuffocata,vt vix ſpiritum ámplius trahere poſſit, nondũ tamen penitus ani-mam exhalauit.Viret.Tract.de Commun. fid.cum Pap.cer. pag.66.67.* The ſumme of his wordes is, firſt,that the popiſh Church may not be accompted of as the *Ma-homet* & *Iewiſh* Churches, which refuſe Chriſt alto-gether: Secondly,that if no prints of Gods Church remayned in the popiſh Church, *Daniel* and *Paul* would not haue foretold: the one,that abomination ſhould be in the Holy place : the other, that *Anti-chriſt* ſhould ſit in the temple of God:Laſtly,that the Church of God amõgſt the Papiſts, though it be al-moſt ſmothered,hath not as yet giuen vp the ghoſt.

Daneus writeth, that the Popiſh Church is the
Church

Church and Temple of God, not fimply, but *fecun-dum quid*, that is, after a fort: His reafon is, becaufe the popifh Church retaineth fome printe of the markes and badges of Gods Church. *Tract. de Ant. cap.17.*

M.Foxe hath thefe words: *Neq̃, enim Romam ita to-tam &c.In Apoc.cap.13.pag.235.* that is,we doe not fo feuer *Rome* frō al felowfhip of the church,that it fhal haue no coniunction at all, with the body of Chrift.

If *M. Penry* miflike my firft reafon, let him con-fute it, &c.

2 *Ieroboam* did fet vp Calues at *Bethel* and *Dan*. In his time, the feruice of God was ftrangely corrup-ted : yet , certaine prerogatiues belonging to the Church,remained then amongft the Iewes.Circum-cifion,which was the Lordes Sacrament, could not be fo defiled by the vncleane hands of the Iewes, but that it was always a figne and Sacrament of Gods couenant : therefore God called the infants of that people,his children,&c.In the Popifh Church,God hath preferued Baptifme,&c.Befides,there remaine amōgft them other remnants, vidz,the Lords pray-er, the Articles of the faith, the Commandements, &c.leaft the Church fhould vtterly perifh,&c. Laft-ly,Almightie God hath miraculoufly preferued a-mongft them the remnants of his people, though poorely and thinly fcattered,&c. Of this M.*Caluine* concludeth, that the popifh Churches, are Chur-ches.*Inftitut.lib.4.cap.2.fect.11.12.*

If my fecond reafon,taken out of M.*Caluine* pleafe you not, confute that part of M.*Caluines* Infti-tutions.

3 If there be no Church at all in Poperie, the in-

V.   fants

fants of Papifts, are not to bee baptized in any *refor-med Church*, though fome of the religiō, doe anfwere for, & vndertake the good educatiō of them. Which I take to be a great errour.

Mafter *Caluine*, and the reft of the learned men in *Geneua*, being required of *M. Knoxe* to fet downe their iudgement, touching this queftion, vidz. whether the infants of Idolaters and excōmunicate perfons might be admitted to baptifme, &c. deliuer this anfwere : *Promiſsio, non ſobolem tantum cuiuſ́q̃ fidelium in primo gradu comprehendit, ſed in mille generationes ex-tēditur. Vnde etiam factum eſt, vt pietatis interruptio, quæ graſſata eſt in papatu, &c. Calu. Epiſt. 285.* The fumme of their words is, that Gods promife, doth not onely comprehend the pofterity of the faithfull in the firft degree, but reacheth vnto a thoufand generations : and that thofe children which defcended of fuch anceftours as were godly many yeeres ago, do belong to the body of the Church, though their parents and grandfathers were Apoftates, &c. *M. Beza* writeth thus of this argument : *Iniquū eſſet Papiſtas, &c. Epiſt. 10.* The fumme of his wordes is, that Papifts are otherwife to bee accompted of then Turkes : becaufe Popery is an aberratiō of the Chriftian Church. Befides, becaufe Gods goodnes extendeth it felfe to a thoufande generations, that it were a hard cafe, to iudge by the profeffion of the later parents, whether the infants pertaine to Gods couenant, &c. Thus farre M. *Beza*.

If any fhall reply, that Gods couenant hath no place at all amongft the Papifts, and therefore that their infants are at no hande to bee baptized in our Churches, howfoeuer fome of the religion offer
them

them in the affemblie to the holy Sacrament: *M.*
Caluines anfwere is : *Cer tum eft, adhuc illic manere refi-*
duum fœdus Dei ex parte: quia quamuis, &c.Cal.Ezec.16.
*20.*That is , It is certaine that the couenant is there
on Gods behalfe,and therfore that Popifh baptifme
needeth not to be renued : befides, that Satan, albeit he raigned oflate in the Popifh Church,could not
altogether extinguifh the grace of God : *imò, illic eſt*
ecclefia. Alioqui,falfum effet Pauli vaticinium , vbi di-
cit,antichriſtum federe in Dei templo. 2. Thef.2.4. That
is, A Church is there : otherwife *Paules* prophecie,
that *Antichriſt* fhould fit in the temple of God, were
falfe,&c. If it fhall pleafe the learned reader to reade
M.*Caluines* Commentarie vpon chap. 16. and verf.
20.of *Ezech*.It will be worth his labour.

A Popifh obiection of the abfurde Papiſts,and
of Maſter Penry.

If the Church of Rome be a Church,thofe Magiftrates which haue feparated themfelues and their fubiects from the Popifh Church, are Schifmatikes,&c.

Anfwere.

Our Magiftrates,people,&c. haue feuered themfelues,not from the Church, but from Idolatry : not
from the common wealth,but from tyranny oppref-
fing the common wealth: not from the Citie, but
from the plague which peſtereth the Citie,&c.that
is, feparation is not frō any trueth remaining in the
Popifh Church, nor from the poore Church, that
is there holden vnder captiuitie , but from the corruptions of the Popifh Church,and from the tyrannie of Antichriſt, which is more grieuous then the
yoke either of *Egypt* or *Chaldæa*: therfore godly princes,&people, cannot iuftly be called Schifmatikes.
Thrafibulus withdrewe himfelfe to *Phile* , during the
V.ij. time

time that thirtie tyrants did teare in peeces the common wealth in *Athens*. *Camillus* withdrew himſelfe
to *Veies*, during the time that the *Gaules* waſted the
Citie of *Rome*. If any ſhal conclude of this, that *Thra-
ſibulus* and *Camillus*, ſeparated themſelues from the
common wealths of *Rome* and *Athens*, and not from
the tyrannie vnder which the *Atheniens* and *Romanes*
then were, hee reaſoneth moſt abſurdly, &c. The
ſumme of my anſwere is conteyned in the writings
of that French Gentleman, *Philip* of *Mornay*. *Tract.
de eccle.cap.10.* The name of Schiſmatike, is much fitter for proud *Penry* and his fantaſtical diſciples, then
for godly Magiſtrates and people, who are moſt ſaw-
cily dealt with, by the Anabaptiſticall crew.

Queſtion.

Whether all our anceſtours, which liued & died in the Popiſh Church,
are damned?

Anſwere.

Philip of *Morney*, doeth anſwere thus: As our ad-
uerſaries make a difference betweene the Church
and the people, ſnatching the name of the Church
onely to the Prelates, which ſhould bee common to
all Chriſtians: ſo, wee likewiſe doe well put a difference, betweene the people cleauing to the Church
of Rome, and the faction of Antichriſt: betweene
them who liue vnder the Popedome, and the vphol-
ders and mainteiners of the Pope: betweene the in-
chaunters, and thoſe that are inchaunted: betweene
the Phariſees, whom Chriſt calleth a generation of
vipers, and the poore ſicke woman, whom he called
the very daughter of Abraham. We ſay, that among
the poore people, which was ſo long time deceiued
vnder the darkeneſſe of Antichriſt, there was a part
of the body of the viſible Church: But that the Pope
and

and his mainteiners, are the botch of the plague in it, which ſtifleth & choketh it as much as it can,&c. And a little after,&c. We knowe that the moſt part of the people, were ignorant of thoſe peſtilent doctrines which the Schoolemen left in writing, that is to ſay, of the principall blaſphemies of the Papacie: alſo, that the more part did neuer beleeue, that they could merite euerlaſting life by their owne workes, whatſoeuer men preached thereof. Againe, albeit that through cuſtome and ignorance they went to Saints and Images, and frequented Maſſes and Pilgrimages: yet notwithſtanding in their conflicts of death, they alwayes principally claue to the croſſe of Ieſus Chriſt. We haue an example of S. *Barnard* himſelfe, and we haue ſeene many more in our time. Saint *Barnard* in certaine places ſauoureth of the contagion of his time, as it was hard hee ſhould doe otherwiſe. But ſee his refuge when hee was tempted of the deuill, in his laſt dayes : *I confeſſe* (ſaith he)*that I am not worthie of it. I knowe that I can not by mine owne workes obteine the kingdome of heauen. But my Lord hath obteyned it by a double right : by inheritance from the father, and by the merite of his paſſion. Nowe he is contented with the one, and giueth me the other. And when I attribute it to my ſelfe, by the gift which he hath made vnto me thereof, I cannot be confounded.* And in another place: *My merite is the mercie of the Lord. And I am not poore in merites, becauſe hee is rich in his mercies : I haue greatly ſinned, but I will comfort my ſelfe in the ſtripes of my Lord.* Euen ſo likewiſe, we aſſure our ſelues in the mercy of God, that a great number helde the foūdation in Ieſus Chriſt, whereof the Apoſtle ſpeaketh, albeit Antichriſt ſhooke it, & as it were, endeuoured to ouer-

turne

turne it in them, all that he might. *Phil.Mor.Tract.de Eccle.cap.9.* Of this iudgement, is that famous man, *Peter Martyr,* in his Commentarie vpon the Epiftle to the *Corinthians,cap.15.verf.18.* I reft in their iudgement.

THAT POPISH PRIESTS

haue a calling, though a faultie one.

F popifh priefts haue no calling at all, Baptifme was deliuered in the Popifh Church by priuate men, which is a groffe abfurditie.

2   Many Popifh Priefts after deteftation of their popifh errours, were allowed minifters in the reformed Churches, without impofition of hands &c. therefore in the iudgement of the beft Churches, they had before a calling though a faultie one.

Thofe execellent fathers and Martyrs, *Cranmer, Rydley, Hooper, Latymer* &c. which were fometimes Popifh priefts, were allowed Minifters of the Gofpel without impofition of hands &c. *Caluine* writing of Popifh priefts hath thefe wordes: *Si verò quis iftufmodi &c.* and a litle after: *Si obijcitur Pauli Canon ille,quo, traditur eligendum Epifcopum irreprehenfibilem effe oportere refpondeo,non hîc agi,meo quidem iudicio, de fimplici vel abfoluta electione,fed de approbatione vel reftitutione ad certum munus, propter interuenientem corruptionem.* And a litle after : *Duo funt in illo ftatu fumma vitia.Vnum,quod non recta ratione inftituti funt ad munus Eeclefiafticum &c.* The fumme of *M. Caluines* words

words is,that fuch Popifh priefts as detefted popery,and were fit to bee employed in the minifterie,
might be allowed,or rather reftored to the Ecclefiafticall function : firft,becaufe they were not before
rightly inftituted. Secondly, *ad corrigendum præce-*
dentem defectum, that is, to correct the former de-
fect &c. *Calu.Epift.373.* By which wordes it is manifeft that Popifh priefts euen in the popifh Church,
had,and haue in M. *Caluines* iudgement a calling,
though a faultie one. The fame M. *Caluine* in an o-
ther place,hath thefe vvordes : *Cogimur fateri penes*
illos effe ordinarium minifterium. that is, We are compelled to confeffe that papifts haue an ordinarie miniftery. *Calu.Ezech:cap.13.v.9.* If M.*Penry* will take
exception againft M.*Caluines* writings & the iudgement of all Gods Churches, let him confute them
very foundly.If he can doe that,he fhal be accopted
the rareft man aliue. If he can not (which I am very
fure of)he fhall not be *Magnus Apollo,*that is,goe for
a Patriarch, (as his ignorant followers do accompt
him) but he fhalbe dubbed(as he is in deede) an o-
ther *Neuius,*that is,a loude and clamorous compa-
nion. If either M. *Penry* or any of his fantafticall
crewe fhall thinke much of my fpeech, I doe not
paffe. I confeffe freely that fharpe wordes are not
fufficient plaifters for fuch proude fores.I hope,the
Magiftrates will confider further of him and fuch
as he is. *Duro nodo,durus cuneus,&c.*that is, A wedge
of yron,is fitteft for knottie vvood.

CHAP.

THEY WHICH ARE ONCE
baptized, must not be baptized againe.

He couenant of grace and peace, which is made and sealed vp in baptisme, is perpetuall: for, Almightie God remaineth euer faithfull in his couenant: therefore, &c.

2 If Baptisme should be iterated, Gods fidelity (which cannot be made voyde by our infidelitie) should be called into question: which were a haynous sinne.

3 Circumcision was neuer iterated, therefore Baptisme may not. Baptisme is to vs, as circumcision was to the Israelites.

4 As the carnall generation is one, so the spirituall generation is one. *Semel nascimur, semel renascimur.*

5 It appeareth not in Gods booke, that any which receiued *baptismum fluminis,* were rebaptized *baptizmo fluminis.*

6 *Agrippinus* the Bishop of *Carthage,* was author of iterating baptisme &c. *Vinc. Lir. Cap.9.*

CHAP. 20.

THERE IS TRVE BAP-
tisme in the Popish Church.

Vch as were and are baptized in the popish Church, were and are engraffed by baptisme into a true Christ: therefore they receiued true Baptisme.

The

The argument followeth: for baptifme is an engraffing into the true Chrift.*Rom.chap.6.3.* The Antecedent is manifeft in M. *Penries* iudgement : for he will not haue them to offer themfelues againe to baptifme: therefore he is either a Catabaptift , or els there was and is (euen in his iudgement) true baptifme in the popifh Church.

2   They which were circumcifed in the time of *Ieroboam* and *Caiphas*,were accompted true circumcifed perfons , although at that time the ftate of the Church was almoft altogether peruerted and corrupted : therefore fuch as were and are baptized in the popifh Church &c. This argument is vfed of the greateft learned men of the religion , and is allowed of all the *reformed Churches.*

3   *Caluine* and *Beza* are refolute for this. *Calu. Ion : chap: 1.v.16.Ezech: 16.v.20.Epift: 103.*and *104. Beza Confeff.chap.4. Art: 49.* and *chap:7. Art: 11.Epift.10.*and *81.*

Viretus hath thefe words:*Baptifmum qui à facerdotibus Papifticis collatus eft,&c.*that is,we do allow popifh Baptifme, albeit we condemne the vaine and fuperftitious ceremonies,which are vfed in it. *Tract.de cōmun. fid.cum Papift.cer.pag.64.*

Of this iudgement are all learned men, and all *reformed Churches.* None diffent, but *Catabaptifts, Anabaptifts, M.Penry,* and the reft of the fantafticall order.

X.   CHAP.

THERE HATH BENE AND
may be true Baptisme out of the Church.

He *Donatists* thought otherwise in *Augustines* time: but they are notably cōfuted by *Augustine* in his bookes, *de baptif.contra Don.*

2 True Circumcision was amongst the Edomites.

3 They which were baptized out of the Church by heretikes, neither were nor might be rebaptized: therefore they receiued true baptisme.

The Antecedent is manifest, for it is a rule in Diuinitie, and receiued of all learned men : *Baptizati ab hæreticis, non sunt rebaptizandi*, that is, they which are baptized of heretickes, are not to be rebaptized.

The reasons are.

Where the essentiall forme of baptisme is obserued, *non hæreticus, sed hæretici manu Christus baptizat.* that is, not the hereticke but Christ doth baptize by the hand of the hereticke. *Aug.passim.de bapt.cōt.Don.*

It is not the baptisme of hereticks or schismaticks, but of God & the Church, wheresoeuer it be found, and whithersoeuer translated. *Aug.de bapt.contra Don. lib.1.cap.14.*

The herefie is theirs : the errour is theirs, &c. but baptisme which is Christes, must not be accompted theirs. *Aug.de baptif.contra Don.lib.3. cap.11.*

Ciprian was of an other iudgemēt in the Church of *Carthage :* but hee was condemned for that errour by the best Churches in that age.

4 The Arke of the testament which was taken of the Philistims, lost not the vertue of Sanctification,

1. Sam.

1.Sam.4. Dagon can teach vs that.

5 *Si foris nemo potest,&c.* that is, if no mã can haue any thing which is Chrifts out of the Church, neither can any man haue any thing which is the deuils within the Church. *Aug.de bapt.contr.Don.lib.4.cap.7.*

6 *Non itaq̃, ideo, non funt facramenta Chrifti & Eccleſia, &c.* that is, they are not therefore, not the Sacraments of Chriſt and the Church, becauſe heretikes and wicked men do vnlawfully vſe them. They, that is, the heretikes, &c. are to be amended or puniſhed: but the Sacraments are to bee acknowledged and reuerently eſteemed of, &c.

Queſtion.

How doe heretikes poſſeſſe baptiſme ?

Anſwere.

Baptiſmum legitimum habent: ſed non legitimè habent: that is, heretikes haue lawful baptiſme, but they haue it not lawfully. *Aug. de Bapt.cont.Don.lib.5.cap.7.Neq̃ licitè foris habetur, & tamẽ habetur: ſic, illicitè foris datur, ſed tamen datur:* that is, Baptiſme is not had lawfully out of the Church: notwithſtanding, it is had: In like ſort, it is giuẽ out of the church vnlawfully: notwithſtanding, it is giuen. *Aug.de Bap.contra Don.lib.6.ca.15.* If any ſhall aske whether it be lawfull to offer our iufants to baptiſme out of the Church, &c. becauſe all learned men (except the Donatiſts, &c. in *Auguſtines* time, and M. *Penry* and his worthie diſciples in our time) haue and doe affirme, that true baptiſme hath bene and may be out of the Church: My anſwere is negatiue, as *Auguſtines* was. I referre the learned reader to his writings *contra Creſc.gram. lib.1. cap.23.* and *de Bapt.contra.Don.lib.1.cap.4.*

X.ij. **CHAP.**

THAT NO POPISH
Prieſt is a Miniſter.

Verie Miniſter muſt bee at the leaſt by profeſſion, a member of the true Church. No Popiſh Prieſt is by profeſſion a member of the true Church. Therefore no Popiſh Prieſt is a miniſter

Euery miniſter hath an office within the body of the Church. No popiſh prieſt hath an office within the body of ẙ Church. Therfore no popiſh prieſt is a miniſter.

The propoſitions or firſt part of both theſe reaſons are ſet down euidently and plainly by the wiſdome of God, in theſe words. For as we haue many members in one body, and all members haue not one office: ſo we being many, are one body in Chriſt, and euery one anothers members, ſeeing then that we haue gifts that are diuers. &c.

The place ſheweth cleerely, that whoſoeuer is not a member, is not of the bodie, if not of the bodie, then no miniſter. Againe, whoſoeuer is no member, he hath no office in the bodie: if no office, no miniſter. He that ſhould obieſt that in this place is ment a member of the bodie, by election in the ſecrete counſell of God, and not in the acknowledgement of the Church by profeſſion, would not deſerue the anſwering. Becauſe it is vocation and not election, that maketh ſuch a member in the Church as may haue an office therein: of which ſort the Apoſtle ſpeaketh in this place. By vocation, I meane that whereof the holy Ghoſt ſpeaketh, where it is ſayde, Many are called, but fewe are choſen: neither can any man denie him to be a member of the Church, which by outward profeſſion ſubmitteth himſelfe vnto true religion, and ſuch are the members, whereof the Apoſtle ſpeaketh: namely ſuch as are members in the iudgement of the Church. Iudas was a member in the iudgement of the Church, though not belonging to election. A further proofe of the propoſitions you ſhall find 1. Cor. 12.26.28. Hee was no prieſt in the olde Teſtament, that was not a Iewe by profeſſion: yea, and of the line of Aaron too: and ſhall he be accounted a miniſter among vs, that is a ſtrãger from the profeſſion of the trueth, and a profeſſed Idolater? Iſhmael and Eſau were circumciſed, and the ſonnes of thoſe fathers vnto whome the couenant was made: Euen I will bee thy God, and the God of thy ſeed. They and their poſterities fell from true religion: well, admit that the profanation of circumciſion had ſtill continued in their houſes: yet a man ſupplying the place of a prieſt among them, was no prieſt in deed, though he ten thouſand times profaned circumciſion, & would brag neuer ſo often, that he worſhipped after his Idolatrous maner, no other God but the God of his father Abraham, and ſware onely by the feare of his father Iſaac. The reaſon hereof is, becauſe that euery prieſt vn-

der

der the law,muſt be an Iſraelite by profeſſion,that is,a member of the true Church, neither could any of the godly aſſure themſelues, that an Edomitiſh prieſt admiſtred true circumciſion according to the ſubſtance. Now I reckon of a popiſh prieſt no otherwiſe thē I would haue done of an Iſmaelitiſh or Edomitiſh circumciſer : the profanation of that ſeale of the couanant,ſtill continuing in mount Seir.

R. Some.

Your Maior propoſitions in your two firſt arguments are. viz. Euery Miniſter muſt bee at the leaſt by profeſſion a member of the true Church. And, euery Miniſter hath an office within the body of the Church. My anſwere is,that your Maior propoſitions,and the proofe of them out of the 12. to the *Rom.* are true,if you giue them this ſenſe, viz. that euery lawfull and good Miniſter of God is by profeſſion a member and hath an office within the body of the ſound Church. If you vnderſtand your Maior propoſitions otherwiſe,I deny them:my reaſon is : Excommunicated heretiques which adminiſter true baptiſme out of the Church, had a calling though a faultie one : and yet theſe heretiques, neither were mēbers, nor had any office in the true Church.That *Iudas* was a veſſel of wrath,and yet an Apoſtle and a member of the Church in the iudgement of the Church,I make no queſtion. The caſe of many hypocrites,hath & may be ſuch for reprobation and miniſterie,though not for Apoſtleſhip. That which I like of in this Treatiſe of yours, I will either alow by ſome ſhort ſpeach, or elſe paſſe ouer with ſilence. Cauiling and wrangling,become not ſuch as profeſſe and loue the Religion. If none may be a Miniſter in Gods Church by Gods order, but ſuch as are members,that is, engraffed into Gods Church: it is a good conſequent that none in the

X.iii. time

time of the Law, might be a Leuiticall Prieſt which
was vncircumciſed. Which point you dealt very
ſtrãgly in before. It is true that none might be a Leuiticall prieſt, which was not a Iewe by profeſſion,
and of the line of *Aaron:*but yet not euery one of *Aa-*
rons line(if he were vnfit for that holy fũctiõ)might
be admitted to the *Leuiticall* prieſthood,as you gaue
out before very abſurdly. No popiſh Prieſt (as hee
is a popiſh Prieſt) is accompted a Miniſter in our
Church.If you thinke otherwiſe, you thinke amiſſe:
for I can aſſure you, that none which haue bene popiſh Prieſtes, either did or doe adminiſter in our
Church without the allowance of our Church. I
confeſſe, they receiue not impoſition of handes a-
gaine either in our Church or in other reformed
Churches. If Circumciſion was amongſt the *Iſma-*
elites and *Edomites* (as you write and I affirme) then
a Sacrament was amongſt them.I pray you remember this. The Prieſtes of *Idumea,* I graunt, were not
Prieſtes in deede, that is, they were not lawfull and
good Miniſters of God: for they had no lawfull calling : yet they had a calling though a faultie one:
Otherwiſe Circumciſion adminiſtred by them had
bene no Sacrament. That which deceiueth you,is,
that you do not diſtinguiſh betweene a lawfull and
good Miniſter of God, and a Miniſter : betweene a
lawfull calling, and a calling,&c.

I.Penry.

Whereas in the aſſumption or ſecond part of both the reaſons, I deny
popiſhPrieſts to be members of the Church:my meaning is not that there
are none of the elect, within the body of Popery,whom the Lord may cal
in his good time : For I woulde not deny this vnto Mahometiſme,or that
there are not left in Popery certaine rubiſhes & ſteps of true Religion, for
this difference I make betwene them and other Infidels,though the Iewes
                                                              alſo

alfo may claime this vnto themfelues. But I meane that the Popifh religion is fuch a religion as whofoeuer liueth & dieth in the profeffion thereof: he liueth and dieth out of the Church, where faluation is not poffibly to be had , for any thing that is made knowen vnto man. Whence it neceffarily foloweth,that in Popery there is no Church.If it be obiected that the Papifts are within the Couenant, inafmuch as long fince they profeffed the trueth : Mine anfwere will be, that Popery was neuer the trueth as yet, that no Papift in that hee was a Papift, euer profeffed the trueth, and that God made no Couenant with profeffed Idolaters,as all Papifts are.

R .Some.

Your Minor propofitions in your two firft arguments are,viz. No popifh prieft is by profeffion a mēber of the church : And,No popifh prieft hath an office within the bodie of the Church.My anfwer is: If by (*church*) in your Minor propofitiōs you meane a found Church : I grant that no popifh prieft (as he is a popifh prieft and a profeffed papift) is either a member by profeffion , or hath an office within the bodie of the Church. If by (*Church*) you meane an vnfound Church : My anfwer is, that a popifh prieft is a member & hath an office within the body of the church.My reafon is:the popifh church is a church, though an vnfound church.For proofe of this I haue vfed diuerfe reafons in this Treatife. I referre you to them.If they wil not downe with you,you muft confute the feuerall writings of *Caluine* in his Inftitutions,Commentaries and Epiftles,& of other famous men,and condemne the iudgement of all the reformed churches.If your ftomacke ferue you,you haue matter inough to work on,& more thē you were wel aware of. That fteps of true Religion remaine in the Popifh Church, it is manifeft : for God preferued in that Church *verbum fuum & baptifmum,* That is, his Word and Baptifme: *Beza in Annot.Matt.23.2.* Yea, we of the Religion haue receiued many good things

from

from the papifts,as the *Ifraelites* did the Arke frō the *Philiftines*. I graunt that the *Iewes* haue many good things amōgft them:yet there is great difference betwene *Iewes* & papifts.The papift receiueth the new Teftamēt : fo doth not the Iew. The papift doth not vfe circūcifion,becaufe the date of it is out,but baptifme which is an engraffing into Chrift. The Iewe retaineth circumcifion & doth not admit baptifme. That the papifts are not altogether aliens frō Gods couenant, I haue fhewed before, and doe reft in *M. Caluines* iudgement, for that point. You write that poperie was neuer the trueth as yet. If you meane that all poperie was neuer the trueth as yet, I agree with you. If you meane that no part in poperie was euer the trueth as yet,you erre groffely,and are refuted by your owne words,which are , that there are certaine fteppes of true religion in poperie.You giue out that no papift (in that he was a papift)euer profeffed the trueth. My anfwere is, that they did and doe erre in very many things, but yet they did and doe profeffe fome trueth : and I doubt not, but that many which liued and died in the time of popifh darkeneffe, died Gods feruants. If you thinke that a man being wide in many things, is wide in all things:then becaufe you,M. *Penry*, haue deliuered manie blafphemous, Anabaptifticall, and other errours, I might iuftly conclude that you hold nothing foundly: but I wil not offer you fuch meafure. If I did,I fhould deale abfurdly with you. Howe profeffed papifts are Idolaters,appeareth in my fecond propofition,which is newly added to my former treatife. Thither I referre you.

I.Penry.

Antichrift I grant fhould fit as God in the temple of God, but it was neuer

uer the temple of God,fince he planted his peſtilent chaire therein. Poperie in deed hath inuaded the ſeates and poſſeſſions of true religion,and began firſt where the trueth was profeſſed. For the myſterie of iniquitie firſt
appeared within the Church,and not elſe-where,where true religion flou-
riſhed, and not among the heathen: neither could he bee that aduerſarie,
whoſe beginning ſhoulde bee in Paganiſme. But although Poperie tooke
roote in the ſoyle where the true Churche was planted: yet it ſo grewe
there, that it ſtill continued to be the ſynagogue of Satan,and could neuer
as yet be the Church of God: howſoeuer it hath ouergrowen the poſſeſſion thereof. And what though their fathers, who now are Papiſts, were
within the couenant, as profeſſing true religion: ſhall it therefore followe
that their Idolatrous ſonnes ſhould be ſo too?If they returne the Lord hath
mercie in ſtore for them I denie not. But what is there in this poynt ſaide
for the Papiſts, which the Iewes cannot with farre more ſhewe of reaſon
pretend for themſelues? The profaning of Baptiſme among the Papiſtes
can make them no more be within the Church, then the continuance of
the profanation of Circumciſion among the Iſhmaelites and Edomites
could keepe them vnder the couenant. And why ſhould popiſh Baptiſme
any more tye the Lords couenant to an Idolatrous race,then an Iſhmaeli-
tiſh or Edomitiſh cutting off of the foreskinne, linke him to be the God of
thoſe adulterous generations? Oh but the Lord himſelfe hath ſaid,In Iſaak
ſhall thy ſeede be called, and Iaacob haue I loued, and hated Eſau. Why
the ſame Lorde in reſpect of his reuealed will, for with his ſecrete election
men muſt not meddle,hath ſayd,the profeſſours of true religion do I loue,
but the Idolatrous papiſts my ſoule abhorreth: It will be here demaunded
whether I make no more account of popiſh baptiſme, then of an Edomitiſh circumciſion,I ſee no reaſon why I ſhould. For a circumciſed Edomite
being receiued,to be a true worſhipper at Ieruſalem,ſhould as well content
himſelfe with that circumciſion(circumciſion being not a thing inuented
by man,or done in reſpect of man,but ordeyned by the Lord, and done in
regard of the couenant made vnto Abraham) as we doe with popiſh baptiſme,which is not called in queſtion.

And yet that which is ſpoken concerning the profeſſion of the trueth,
by the forefathers, is not altogether true in popery: for there bee many
large regions nowe profeſſing poperie, where not ſo much as the name
of Chriſt was heard,vntill they were become groſſely popiſh. So that their
firſt ſtep was out of paganiſme vnto poperie. And this is the eſtate of all
thoſe poore oppreſſed vaſſals the weſt Indians,who now in great numbers
profeſſe Romiſh Idolatrie.For at ſuch time as the Spanyard inuading their
land, brought vpon them the moſt miſerable ſlauerie of the body & ſoule,
that are vpon any people vnder heauen, they had not ſo much as hearde
whether there was any Chriſt,but were moſt heathniſh,and ſenceleſſe Idolaters, as may appeare by the popiſh hyſtoriographers themſelues, who
wrote the ſtories of thoſe tymes.And therefore (to omit, whoſe poſterities
many of the nations within Europe are, that haue refuſed the light of the
Goſpel)though it were granted,that the reſt of the popiſh rable were with-

in the couenant: yet thefe miferable heathen papifts, can be faid to be vnder no couenant, but that which is made vnto popery and paganifme. I
hope M.*Some*, howfoeuer you may be perfwaded, that other popifh fhaue-
lings can deliuer a facrament, yet that you will doubt, whether any man
could be affured to receyue thofe holy feales at the hands of the heathen
maffemongers remayning in Cuba, Hyfpaniola, Mexico, or any other the
Eafterne parts.

    And thus much concerning the affumption. I am not ignorant that fa-
mous and worthie men, haue otherwife written concerning the popifh
Church, and therefore I am not to be preffed with their authoritie.

R.Some.

If your writings were as founde as they are abfurde, they would giue many times great aduantage
to the Papift, Anabaptift, &c. If the popifh church
was neuer the temple of God, fince *Antichrift* planted his peftilent chaire there, then in your iudgement, the Pope is not *Antichrift:* for *Antichrift* doth
and muft fit in the Temple of God, that is, in the
Church of God. I haue handled this argument before. I reft in that I haue written there. You fay
that a circumcifed *Edomite* being receiued into the
Church of *Ierufalem*, fhould content himfelfe with
his circumcifion in *Idumea*, becaufe circumcifion
was the Lords ordinance &c. I agree with you in
this. If the Edomitifh circumcifion was the Lords
ordinance, then it was a feale of Gods couenant to
the *Idumeans*, and confequently the *Edomites* in
your iudgement were not Aliens from Gods couenant: for, the feale of the couenant, doth import and
prefuppofe a couenant. Befides, if the Edomitifh
circumcifion was true circumcifion, and the Edomitifh Church no Church : then a Sacrament was
out of the Church &c. How like you this, M. *Penry*?
You knowe my meaning. You adde, that you call
not popifh baptifme in queftion. Here, I grant, you
doe not : but a little after, you vfe thefe wordes : viz.

where there is no true Chrift wherunto men can be
engraffed by baptifme, there true baptifme as touching the fubftance cannot be gotten &c.But in popery there is no trueChrift &c .*mendacem oportet effe
memorē*.Your memory is very fhort.You would neuer,I thinke, haue vēted fuch motley ftuffe as this, if
you had thought it would haue bin looked on. I can
affure you,that befides me,whom you haue put to a
litle paines, your treatife hath beene viewed and re-
uiewed by very many learned men,who condemne
it for a foolifh and fantafticall bable. If the weft
Indians after profeffion of their beliefe in the holy
trinitie,were baptized,as you fay, by popifh fhaue-
lings,I affure my felfe that they receiued true baptifme,& were therfore engraffed into Chrift.We in
the Church of *England* neede not faile(thanks be to
God)to the maffemōgers in *Cuba, Hiſpaniola, Mexico*,or any other part of the *Indians*, we haue Gods
holy feales amongft vs.If you cal fuch of the *Indians*
as are baptized,heathen,you do them great wrong:
for baptifme is the externall badge of a Chriftian.
I doe not maruaile though you bee bolde with the
Indians,which are fo farre off,when you are fo faucy
with the principal of the religion in this noble land:
I meane our Magiftrates and learned men, which
are finguler ornaments ofour Church & common-
wealth. The queftion you mooue,fhall receiue my
anfwere,when I vnderftand that either you or fome
other of your fantafticall difciples, are on fhippe-
boarde,& vnder faile for *Mexico* in *India*. You confeffe that famous men haue written otherwife of the
popifh Church then you thinke. To that ende you
quote M.*Caluines* 103.Epiftle. I reft in his iudgement:

ment: becaufe you doe not fo, I pray you confute him. I muft needes tell you plainely that I make more accompt of one *Caluine* then of a thoufand *Penries*. *Caluine* was a man of finguler learning, an enemie to papifts, Anabaptifts, Catabaptifts, &c. a notable light and ornament in Gods Church. What you are,I will not fay.I would be loth to doe you wrong: therefore,I will not match you with fo famous a man as M.*Caluine* was.

I.Penry.

I might in the third place vfe againft you M.*Some*,a reafon of your owne thus concluded. No minifterie is facriledge,becaufe euery minifterie is an ordinance of God,which cannot bee turned vnto facriledge. The popifh prieſthood is facriledge,as you haue fet downe 21. Therefore the popifh priefthoode is no miniftery, and confequently popifh priefts are no minifters.You may fee that you haue ouerthrowen your owne caufe. But this maner of reafoning,although it fhould be of force agaynft your felfe, inafmuch as your owne wordes are brought to expreffe your owne meaning, yet I account infufficient.

R.Some.

I haue written, I confeffe, that the Popifh priefthood is facriledge.Of this you cōclude, that the popifh Priefthood is no Minifterie,that is,no calling at all: and that I haue ouerthrowen mine owne caufe. Stay your felfe a while good Sir. This victory deferueth not fo much as an oaten ftraw for the trumpet. I denie your argument: for it is a fallace *à fecundum quid ad fimpliciter*.I graūt that that part of the Popifh priefthood which is occupied in facrificing, is facriledge: But that part of the Popifh priefthood which is occupied in the adminiftration of baptifme is not facriledge. For this point I allow *Chemnicius* iudgement,His words are thefe:*Verum quidem eſt,quia principalis pars miniſterij eſt doĉtrina : quod ideo quando vera doĉtrina deprauatur,& praua opiniones ſtabiliuntur,ipſum miniſterium mutatur, & quod iĺ̆oru miniſterium,qui do-*
ĉtrinam

ctrinam corrumpunt, ideo reliquendum fit, quia ſcriptum eſt: Cauete à pſeudoprophetis: Item, vocem alienorum non audiunt, ſed fugiunt ab ea. Simul tamen & hoc verum eſt, partem miniſterij, vt ſacramenti alicuius adminiſtratio-nem, aliquando poſſideri etiam ab his, qui in alijs materijs graues errores amplectûtur: imò ſæpe habent, adminiſtrant, & dant vera ſacramenta illi etiam, qui ipſis ſacramentis aſ-ſuunt falſas aliquas opiniones, modò ſubſtantialia, quæ ad materiam & formam iuxta inſtitutionem pertinent, ſer-uent: ſicut exemplum de circumciſione Caiphæ, Scribarum & Phariſæorum manifeſtè teſtatur. Nullo modo autem ſe-quitur, quia vera fuit circumciſio, quæ à Phariſæis dabatur, ideo etiam veras fuiſſe omnes opiniones, quas præter & con-tra verbum Dei, non tãtum alijs articulis doctrinæ, verum ipſi etiã circumciſioni, traditionibus ſuis aſſuebant. Chemn. in 2.par.exam.decret. Conc. Trident: Canon. 5. The ſumme of his wordes is, that though true doctrine which is the principall part of the Miniſterie be de-praued, yet that a part of the miniſterie, viz. the ad-miniſtration of a Sacrament, is poſſeſſed ſometimes of them which in other matters hold groſſe errours. Yea, they haue and do often adminiſter a Sacrament (though they do annexe to the Sacramẽt ſome falſe opinions) if they reteine ſuch things according to the Inſtitution, which bee eſſentiall for matter and forme. Circumciſion vſed in the time of *Caiphas* and the *Phariſes*, is witneſſes ynough of this, &c. Thus you ſee how trimly my wordes do ſerue your turne. *Thraſilaus* was a fráticke man amongſt the *Athenians*. He counted all the ſhips which ſailed towardes *A-thens*, to be his: but he was fouly deceiued: ſo are you in accompting my ſpeaches your arguments.

Priesthood of our sauour Christ: But the verie ministery of popish priests;
directly ouerthroweth the Priesthoode of Christ : therefore they are no
ministers.

I knowe not what can be pretended agaynst the proposition,vnlesse men
would dreame of a ministery, with whom the Priesthood of the Lorde Iesus cãnot stand. The latter part of the reason is true,if it be true that Christ
is the only sacrifice for sinne,that he is no more to be offered,that by once
offering himselfe,he hath made ful satisfaction for the sinnes of the whole
world,and that the popish priests dayly sacrifice to appease Gods wrath,
for the sinnes of the quicke and the dead.

R. Some.

Before that I answere this Argument, I must tell
you first,that euery one of the Religion is perswaded
(as well as you) that Christ is the onely sacrifice for
sinne. Secondly,I must tell you, that this argument
of yours is very neare of kinne to that which you wil
needes borow of me : for it is al one with the last. But
I must beare with you: you haue a speciall gift in va-
rying a phrase. For that,you shall beare the Bell,and
cary the clapper too,if you wil. Is any part,I beseech
you,of the Popish priesthoode, called sacriledge by
any learned Protestãt,but becaufe it is occupied (as
the Papistes say most abfurdly) in sacrificing Christ?
Nowe I come to your worthy reason. I denie your
Minor. My reason is as before.I rest in my answer to
your former argument, which is the fame with this.
Nowe Sir,if I were difpofed as you are, I could giue
out,that you are neere driuen,when one Argument
appeareth(I wil not fay as you did,is periured)twife:
and that you are like to them which woulde make
men beleeue,there are feuerall meates, becaufe one
kinde of meate is ferued in feuerall difhes.

I. Penry.

Lastly, they are no Ministers who are made, that is, called, elected and
ordeined by Idolaters. Popish priests are called, chosen and ordayned by
Idolaters : Therefore they are no ministers.

The

The propofition appeareth,in that a minifter can be made by none, but by fuch as vnto whom the Lord hath giuen leaue to deale in that action,otherwife the action is fruftrate. As if a company of women, though religious and godly,fhould go about to make a minifter, the action is nothing. Of the affumption that popifh prieftes are made by Idolaters, I make no queftion. And when did God giue Idolaters leaue to make minifters?

Seeing therefore that popifh priefts are no minifters, I fee no fhewe of probabilitie whereupon my faith,or the faith of any can be affured to receyue true baptifme at their hands : vnleffe it can bee fhewed by you, M. *Some*,that eyther there may bee fayth where there is no promife, or that there is a promife to recciue a facrament where there is no minifter,which no man of any chriftian modeftie will affirme.Hence alfo it followeth,that neither the obftinate crew of recufants in this land, who offer their children to bee profaned by trayterous and runnagate Iefuites, nor any elfe within the body of the Romifh Babylon,can affure themfelues that their children receyue the fubftance of baptifme.

R. Some.

If by minifters in your Maior propofition, you meane lawfull and good minifters of God, I agree with you.If you meane otherwife,I diffent.If by idolaters in your Maior propofitiō,you vnderftand not Pagane but popifh idolaters: my anfwere is, that fuch as were called, elected and ordained by them, had a calling though a faultie one. Otherwife *Luther,Ridley,Cranmer,Hooper,&c*.had no calling at all. For this point,I referre you to that I haue fet downe before,*chap.1 8*.of this Treatife. You aske this queftion,viz. When did God giue idolaters leaue to make minifters? I anfwere: euen then when he gaue the Ifraelites leaue to make your ignorant Leuites priefts: and when hee gaue foolifh electours of Magiftrates leaue to chufe fuch Magiftrates as your foole *Candaules* was : that is, Almightie God gaue no leaue at all. And yet you are refolute, that the ignorant Leuitical priefts,which might be wel begged for idiots were lawfull prieftes,though not good prieftes :and that fuch as are chofen Magiftrates euen againft the

wooll,

wooll, haue both the life and birth of Magiſtrates.
It pleaſeth you to ſay, that becauſe Popiſh prieſts are
no miniſters in your iudgement, that you cannot be
aſſured to receiue baptiſme at their hands. Then belike, if you were perſwaded (as all learned men are)
that Popiſh prieſts haue a calling, you would be content that infants ſhould be preſented to baptiſme in
the Popiſh Church: vvhich Popiſh Church in your
iudgement, is no church at all. What I thinke of that
particuler, I vvill not preſently vvrite : but this I tell
you, that this Argument doeth not neceſſarily fol-
low:viz. True circumciſion was giuen in *Idumea,* and
true baptiſme hath bene & may be giuen of excommunicated heretiques : therefore, they of *Ieruſalem*
in the former times, might require circumciſion a-
mongſt the *Edomites,* or they of *Hippo* or *Carthage* in
latter times, might require baptiſme amongſt the
Donatiſts.

I.Penry.

My reaſons beſides that they are no miniſters, are theſe. And I deſire that
they may be examined by you, good M.*Some* , where you muſt remember
that I ſpeake not of that which hath bene done yeſterday, but of the aſſu-
riance that may be had of that which to morow is to be done.

R.Some.

Sir, you deſire me to examine your reaſons. You
ſhall haue an eaſie ſuite of this : for I am very for-
vvarde to doe you that pleaſure. You graunt it to be
baptiſme vvhich vvas adminiſtred yeſterday in the
Popiſh church : but, you doubt of that vvhich is deliuered to morow. Then yeſterday a Sacrament, and
to morovv none. You dare not for your eares, ſay in
flat termes, that it vvas no baptiſme vvhich vvas deliuered heretofore in the Popiſh church : for then,
many thouſandes vvhoſe Chriſtendome you call in
queſtion

queſtion, would condemne you for a *Catabaptiſt*. But
it hath pleaſed you to ſet dovvne this marginal note
in an other place, viz. *As I doe not deny that which hath
bene done to be a Sacramēt: ſo, if any can proue it to be none,
I will not withſtande him. In your Exhort. to the gouernours &c.of Wales, pag.31.* If I vvere not vvell acquainted vvith your abſurd vvritings , I ſhould vvonder at
you more then I doe. Your reaſons, ſuch as they are,
do follovv.

I. Penry.

Where there is no true Chriſt whereunto men can be engraffed by baptiſme, there true baptiſme as touching the ſubſtance cannot bee gotten:
for what baptiſme is that, which is not an ingraffing into the true Chriſt?

But in popery there is no true Chriſt, whereunto men may be ingraffed,
becauſe he is not the true Chriſt, who either will not, or cannot ſatisfie the
wrath of God for the ſinnes of the elect, without their merits, and ſuch is
the Chriſt profeſſed in popery, and no other.

Therefore men cannot be aſſured to haue the ſubſtance of baptiſme in
the popiſh Church.

R. Some.

I denie your Minor propoſition: for ſuch as were
baptized in the Popiſh church, were engraffed by
baptiſme into a true Chriſt. The eſſentiall forme of
baptiſme was and is retained by the Popiſh prieſtes:
viz. *To baptiʒe in the Name of the holy Trinitie.* If your
Minor propoſition were true as it is very falſe : then
very many in this and other landes which were baptized by Popiſh prieſts in the Popiſh church, are vnbaptized: for baptiſme is an engraffing into the true
Chriſt: and you write that no ſuch engraffing is in
the Popiſh church, becauſe no true Chriſt is profeſſed in poperie. If you tell me that you ſpeake not of
that which was done yeſterday, but of that which is
to morowe, it is a blinde and beggerly ſhift : for the
Chriſt profeſſed in poperie, was a deuided Chriſt,

when her Maieſtie was baptized, as euen nowe he is in the Popiſh church. That caſe and profeſſion is all one. To proceede, becauſe I will anſwere your rea-ſon thorowly, I wil ſet it down in this ſort: *The Chriſt profeſſed in Poperie is a deuided Chriſt, and cōſequently not a true Chriſt: therefore none in the Popiſh church are en-graffed by baptiſme into the true Chriſt.* This is your rea-ſon *M.Penry*. My anſwere is, your Antecedēt is true: I denie your argument. My reaſon is: the falſe pro-feſſion of any man whatſoeuer, cānot ſeparat Chriſt from his owne inſtitution, *Rom.3*: therefore, ſeeing Chriſts inſtitution is in Popiſh baptiſme, the true Chriſt is there, that is, in that baptiſme. I doe ſet downe my wordes more warily then I needed: be-cauſe I finde you to be a meere wrangler, and to take vp that which I neuer let fall. Beſides, circumciſion in *Idumea*, as you write, was true circumciſion and a ſeale of Gods couenant: yet, the *Edomites*, which you cannot denie, failed in the true worſhip of Almigh-tie God. I hope you ſee by this time that your Argu-ments are *ſcopæ diſſolutæ*, very looſe ware and ſlender-ly truſſed together. I am ſure you eſteemed them mountaines: but they are not worthie the name of mollhils. I deale plainely with you. If my anſweres pleaſe you not, confute them directly, and not with *ifs, ands,* and *whies:* in which kinde of anſwering (if I may call it anſwering) you haue a ſpeciall grace.

I.Penry.

No man can aſſure himſelfe to haue the ſubſtaunce of baptiſme out of the Church, and that by thoſe that are without the Church: for then a ſa-crament might be had out of the Church, which were very impious and abſurd to be affirmed.

But popery is out of the Church, and ſo are all popiſh prieſts.

Therfore no man can aſſure himſelfe to haue the ſubſtance of baptiſme in poperie by any popiſh prieſt.

R.Some.

R. Some.

Before that I deny any part of your reafon, I muft tell you that I haue proued alreadie that true baptifme hath bene and may be out of the Church. *Ciprian* thought otherwife, and therefore would haue fuch as were baptized by excõmunicated hereticks, to be rebaptized. But he was and is condemned for that errour by ancient & later writers. You giue out very peremptorily, that it is very impious and abfurde to affirme that baptifme either hath bene or may be out of the Church. So did the *Donatifts* in *Auguftines* time. It is no great matter what you fay. Your bolt is foone fhot. Your water is very fhallow. Many points vvhich you condemne in your Confiftorie for groffe abfurdities, are manifeft trueths in the found iudgement of all reformed Churches. So is this prefent particuler. Touching your argument, I denie your Minor. My reafon is: the Popifh church is a church though an vnfound Church: and Popifh prieftes haue a calling though a faultie one. For proofe of this I referre you to that vvhich I haue vvritten before in this Treatife. If you like not my reafons, confute them.

I. Penry.

That there is no Church at all in poperie, and that all popifh priefts are out of the Church, befides the former reafons, this one doth further fhew. If there be a Church in poperie, or if all popifh priefts bee not out of the Church, then thofe magiftrates that haue feparated themfelues and their fubiects (and all others that made this feparation) from the Romifh religion, as from that fynagogue where faluation is not to be had, and confequently, where there is no Church, are fchifmatikes, to fpeake the leaft. Becaufe it is a fchifme to make this feparation from the Church, deteft the corruptions thereof we may, but make fuch a feparation from the Church, we ought not vnleffe we would be accounted fchifmatiks. But thofe Magiftrates and their people, that made this feparation, are not fchifmatickes, becaufe in Poperie the foundation is ouerthrowen. You fay in your booke

Z.ii.   (M.*Some*)

(*M.Some*) page 33.that you could preſſe the Argument of the Magiſtracie againſt me very farre. Whether you may or no,that ſhal be côſidered when I deale with the point: but this I am aſſured of, that in this point,you ſhall be driuen either to defend the abſurditie, that baptiſme is to be had out of the Church in a companie eſtranged from Chriſt, which I thinke you will not do,or vrged ſo farre,as to the plaine breach of a Statute(which farre be it from me)euen in the cauſe of treaſon. Will ye ſay that baptiſme maybe had out of the Church? the aſſertion is abſurd: Or will you hold that there is a Church in Poperie? the aſſertion is dangerous, and I haue prooued it falſe. It is dangerous, becauſe it affirmeth our Magiſtrates to be ſchiſmatiks,inaſmuch as they haue ſeparated themſelues from the Church:I hope rather then you will fall into either of theſe points,that you will graunt me the cauſe.

R.Some.

I will anſwere your ſeuerall pointes very briefly. The reaſon which you vſe to prooue there is no Church at all in popery,is this, viz. If there bee a Church at al in popery,the Magiſtrates and people which are of the religion are ſchiſmaticks at the leaſt. My anſwere is,that this is a popiſh argument. I haue anſwered it before, and doe reſt in that anſwere. If either you or any of the popiſh ſort miſlike my anſwere,you may confute it. Beſides,if there be no Church at all in popery, as you affirme, why ſhould the Churches of *England,Germany,Dēmarke,* (which were ſometimes popiſh)be called *reformed Churches*? The very name of *reformed Churches* doth manifeſtly import, that the Churches of *England,Germanie,Denmarke,* &c. (though popiſh and vnſound)were Churches in ſome ſort, before the reformation. If you thinke that all the popiſh ſorte which died in the popiſh Church ore damned, you thinke abſurdly:for you diſſent from the iudgement of all the learned proteſtants,and doe preſume to ſit in Gods chaire,which is intollerable ſawcineſſe. To ſay,or write,that true baptiſme hath beene, and may bee out of the Church, is a true propoſition

in

in diuinitie. *Augustine* did maintaine it againſt the Donatiſts. The moſt famous mē & Churches in our time, are of that iudgement. I reſt in that with all my heart. You account it an abſurde propoſition. The beſt is, you are not maſter of the ſentences, as *Peter Lumbard* was. If you were (which God defend) the ſoûnde diuinity which is taught in *Cambridge* and *Oxford,*ſhould bee cryed downe, and your ſtrange fancies ſhould be ruled caſes. The argument of the magiſtracy is touched before. I perceiue it hath mooued you a litle : for you drawe out a ſtatute of Treaſō, &c. What, I beſeech you good Sir? No leſſe then Treaſon? youare a charitable man. I haue, do, and will perfourme all dutie, by Gods grace, to the religion and my gracious Prince, ſo long as I liue: therefore treaſon ſtatutes can take no hold of mee. Yea, the refutation of your blaſphemous, Anabap-tiſticall, popiſh, and proude errours by me, is, I am ſure, a performance of a ſpeciall ductie to Almigh-tie God, my Prince, and this Church. And, I doubt not, but that bleſſing which God hath giuen alrea-dy to my laſt treatiſe, and which his Maieſtie will giue to this, will marre your market. Great wordes ſhal not fray me, &c. If your ignorāt diſciples wil ſtil magnifie you, it ſhal not be ſtrāge to me: they do but their kind. Such as bee learned & wiſe, haue, & do find you out. *Cognoſcitur quis ſit, vt vt laudetur Coruus.* The moſt famous orators that euer were in *Rome* and *Athens,* could not make the rauen to be no rauen. *Tertullus* commended *Felix, Act.24.* but *Felix* was an abſurde body, and ſtripped of his office by *Claudius Ceſar.* The Samaritans commended *Simon Magus. Act.8: Libanius* the Sophiſter commended *Iulian*
              Z.iij.   the

the *Apoſtate.Socr.lib.3.cap.* 22. *Eunomius* cōmended *Aetius*, which was a peſtilent heretike. *Theodor.lib* 2.*cap.29*. You haue proteſted many times in your treatiſe that you reuerence me : but here you offer me this choiſe, either to defende that which is in your iudgemēt an abſurditie(but in deede is none) or to incurre the danger of treaſon &c. Doe you thinke that I haue any the leaſt cauſe to beleeue your glorious proteſtations ? *Ioab* pretended extraordinarie good will to *Abner*, and *Amaſa* : but he killed them. *2.Sam.3. and 20.chap*. *Iſmael* pretended extraordinarie good wil to them of *Sichem,Silo, Samaria :* the beaſt ſhedde teares,but they were *Crocodiles* teares : for of 80. godly men hee killed 70. of them.*Ier.cap.41.Iudas* kiſſed Chriſt,but he betrayed him.*Matth.26.* You vſe goodly wordes ſometimes, but proud malice will appeare : it cannot bee hidden. *Marcus Cicero* in his time had many hollow friendes. After his returne from baniſhment,he was reuenged of them *Nihil credendo,omnia cauendo*,that is,in crediting them in nothing, and bewaring of them in euery thing.If I ſerue you ſo, I can not bee iuſtly blamed.You pretende great ſinceritie and innocencie : but your hereticall abſurdities in your treatiſe,and your ſhameleſſe dealing with our Magiſtrates and learned men, doe crie aloude that you are in deede very litle acquainted with ſincerity and innocencie.I tell you plainely,that I like better *Humile peccatum' quàm ſuperbā innocentiam,* that is,humble ſinne then proud innocēcie.The humble Publican was more accounted of then the proude Phariſee.*Luk.18.* I pray God with all my heart to keepe me and all ſuch as loue the religion and deteſt your

Anabap-

Anabaptifticall fancies, from fuch as you and the
fantafticall fort are. You and they are ftrange cattel.
Your hope that I will graunt you the caufe you defend, is a vaine hope : for I thinke great fcorne to be
one of ignorãt *Penries* difciples, that is, a proud and
ignorant Anabaptift. If you will haue any thing at
my hands in diuinitie matters, you muft gaine it by
force of argument. If you thinke that I will come off
otherwife, you are in a wrong boxe: for I intend not
to be at your whiftle. Yea, I require and charge you
in the name of God (if you be not voyde of grace)
to confeffe your ignorance, to deteft your errours,
to yeeld vnto Gods truth, that Gods bleffing may
reft vpon you. If you refufe to doe this, take heede
that Gods vengeance feaze not vpon you.

I.Penry.

Laftly, if men might be affured that they could haue the true fubftance
of baptifme in Popery, then they ought not to keepe their children from
Popifh baptifme, if there were no other baptifme in the worlde to be had.
For men might come to their baptifme & deteft their corruptions, if it be
Gods baptifme, as you *M.Some* affirmed it to be, pag 20. And they can adde
an edifying worde vnto the Sacrament : if the recitall of the wordes of inftitution be an edifying word, and that be fufficient to make a Sacrament,
both which you haue written, page 23.24. But men ought rather to keepe
their children vnbaptized, then to offer them to bee prophaned by Popifh
baptifme, both for the former reafons, and becaufe wee ought to haue no
more fellowfhip with Papifts in the feruice of God, then with Pagane idolaters. *M.Caluine* hath written otherwife in this point, therefore againe I
appeale to the word.

R.Some.

I vvill anfvvere this fection of yours both briefly
and roundly by the grace of God. That baptifme deliuered in the Popifh church, was and is Gods baptifme, I make no queftion. For proofe of this point, I
haue fet downe waightie reafons in my former treatife: One of *M.Caluines*, an other *ab Abfurdo*. Your anfweres to them are very foolifh, and are fo accounted

ted of by the learned fort.I haue examined them a litle in this Treatife. It is the iudgement of all the reformed Churches, that there was & is true baptifme
in the Popifh church.Before, you denied it not: but
now, the cafe is altered: you accompt it an errour to
affirme it.What mutabilitie is this? Hee that would
faile after your compaffe for Diuinitie matters,
fhould proue as giddie as a goofe. I pray God with
all my heart to bleffe his people in *England* & *Wales*,
and to keepe them from fuch blinde guides as the ignorant fort are, and from fuch fhameleffe and fantafticall guides as you, *M.Penry*, are. Concerning this
queftion, viz.whether men ought to offer their children to Popifh baptifme, if there were no other baptifme in the world to be had: *M.Penry* faith one while
that they ought, if Popifh baptifme be Gods Baptifme : which before he denied not. An other while,
he is peremptory that mē ought rather to kepe their
childrē vnbaptized.His reafon is : becaufe we ought
to haue no more fellowfhip with papifts in Gods
feruice, then with pagane Idolaters.The iffue therefore nowe is : firft, whether infants ought rather to
be kept vnbaptized, then to bee prefented to popifh
baptifme. Secondly, whether no more fellowfhip
is to be had with papifts in Gods feruice, then with
heathen Idolaters. Concerning the firft queftion,
M.*Caluines* refolution is affirmatiue, if the parents
(which they cannot do without peril of life) do publikely deteft the popifh corruptions. M.*Caluines* reafon is : the omitting of baptifme is contempt of
Chriftianitie. *Cal.Epift.104.*Of this iudgement are
Melanchthon and *Peter Martyr.Cal.Epift.103.& Viretus Tract : de commun : fid.cum papift.Cer.pag.61,62,70.*
I con-

I confeſſe freely, that this is a very waightie queſtion (but in this our time a needeleſſe queſtion) and that men of great excellécie for learning, haue their ſeueral iudgements. I would be loath to ſtirre coales in this argument. Touching the other queſtion, M. *Penry* ſaith that no more fellowſhip is to be had in religion matters with papiſts then with pagane Idolaters. I diſſent from him in this. My reaſons are: firſt, the papiſts profeſſe the holy Trinitie: ſo doe not the pagane Idolaters. Secondly, the papiſts are not altogether aliens from Gods external couenant: but the heathen Idolaters as yet are. Laſtly, M. *Caluine* is very flat againſt you in this point. *Epiſt.104.* In ſteed of anſwering his reaſons in that Epiſtle, you appeale to the word. A ſtrange kindof appealing, whẽ M. *Caluines* arguments are drawen out of the holy word. If you wil deale plainly as you ought, neuer piddle any longer: goe through ſtitch withall: ſeeing you are ouer ſhoes, aduenture ouer bootes too: confute *Caluines 104. Epiſtle*, and that which he hath written very excellently vpon the *20.verſe* of the *16.chap. of Ezechiel*. If you giue the vnſet, and fayle (whereof I make no queſtion) you ſhall loſe no credite of learning: for you neuer had any as yet. *Qui ſemel verecundiæ limites &c.* you knowe the reſt.

I.Penry.

Seeing therfore in Popery there is no Church, no Miniſtery, no Chriſt: Seeing we ought in no caſe to be ioyned with Papiſtes in their religion, but to be ſeparated from them, as from thoſe that are out of the Church, and ſuch as are become a very filthy cage and neſt of vncleane and ſacrilegious idolaters: therefore alſo it neceſſarily followeth, that neither our Popiſh recuſants, nor any elſe, offring their children to be baptized in the Popiſh ſynagogue, by thoſe polluted and vncleane Prieſtes, may aſſure themſelues that they can bee there partakers of true baptiſme, as touching the ſubſtance of baptiſme.

A a.   R.Some.

R.Some.

Seeing therefore in the iudgement of all learned men and all reformed Churches, there is in popery, a Church, a Miniſtery, a true Chriſt into whom very many haue bene and are engraffed by Baptiſme: it is a ſure conſequent, firſt that you haue kept ſträge coyles in comptrolling all the Churches of God, and in ſetting downe arguments as cleare as midnight: Secondly, that your concluſion (viz. that there is in popery, no Church, no miniſtery, no Chriſt) is nothing elſe but an Anabaptiſticall flouriſh, which will melt as waxe before the fire, and vaniſh as ſmoke before the wind.

CHAP. 24.

R.Some.

Efore that I ſet downe M. *Penries* propoſition & reaſons touching vnpreaching Miniſters, I muſt tell the godly reader, firſt, that my iudgement is, that Almighty God neuer called any to the holy miniſterie, either in the old or new Teſtament, but he gaue them gifts fit for that holy funſtion: Secondly, that by *vnpreaching Miniſters*, I vnderſtand ſuch as haue gifts in no meaſure, for the diſcharge of that holy funſtion. Such are M. *Penries* ignorant Leuiticall prieſts, whom he warranteth (notwithſtanding their extreeme ignorance) to be lawfull prieſts, though not good prieſts. Such are ſome in our dayes, which are fitter for the belfray, then for the bodie of the Church. That ſuch as theſe are, and they which admitted them, ſinned groſſely, I make no queſtion. That ſuch ignorant

men

men ought to bee thruſt out of the holy miniſterie, and ſent to ſome occupation , is a cleare and ruled caſe in Gods booke. I haue handled this argument before : I reſt in that which I haue written there.

I. Penry.

That ⁀vnpreaching miniſters are no miniſters.

They are affirmed to bee no Miniſters, not becauſe they are euill miniſters, but becauſe their Miniſterie is an euil and profane miniſterie: So that in this point the fault is not found with the euill miniſter, but with the euill miniſterie. Their miniſterie is prophane and euill, becauſe there is no mention made of it in the worde. And a miniſtery not mentioned in the worde is no miniſtery, but a prophane conſtitution. For the Lord hath expreſly ſet downe euery miniſtery of the newe Teſtament, that ſhould be in the Church vnto the worlds ende : Whereas he hath not once mentioned the Miniſterie of our Readers, becauſe it is not a preaching Miniſtery. The ſumme of this whole controuerſie is conteined in theſe three axiomes.

　1　Euery miniſtery is expreſly ſet downe in the word.

　2　Euery miniſtery of the newe Teſtament is a preaching miniſtery.

　3　The miniſtery of our vnpreaching miniſters, is not a preaching Miniſtery.

If you can ſhewe either of theſe 3. points to be falſe, I am ouerthrowen: if neither, you muſt yeelde. The trueth of all three, I haue ſhewed out of the Worde, in the laſt edition of my booke. The two former are confirmed by the places quoted on the margent.

R. Some.

My anſwere ſhall be ſo briefe as may be. Wherein I diſſent, I will giue my reaſons. If the miniſterie (as you ſay) of vnpreaching miniſters be an euil and profane miniſterie, it is a good conſequent, that vnpreaching miniſters, are euill and profane miniſters. The argument foloweth *à coniugatis*. To proceede: you write, that the miniſterie of ignorant miniſters, is not mentioned in the word : therefore it is no miniſterie (in your iudgement) but a profane conſtitution. I am ſure you thinke this argument to be a ſure

one, but you are fowly deceyued. I deny your antecedent. My reafon is : By *Minifterie* in your antecedent, I vnderftand *the reading of the holy Scriptures, the
deliuering of the publikee prayers, the adminiftration of the
Sacraments:* all which are the cõftitution of Almightie God, therefore no profane conftitution, as you
verie profanely doe imagine. He that mifliketh the
reading of the holy Scriptures, is a *Zwingfildian* heretike. He that mifliketh the adminiftration of the
Sacraments, is a *Meffalian* heretike. He that mifly-
keth the inuocation of our gracious God, is a filthie
Atheift, that is, of no religion. If you tell me, that
you thinke excellently of the adminiftration of the
Sacraments, publique prayers, &c. But that your
meaning is, that it is not Gods pleafure, that ignorant men fhoulde adminifter fuch precious iewels,
I affent vnto you : but, I muft adde this, that as you
and I doe miflike the entrance of vnfit men into, and
the continuance of them in the holy minifterie, fo
neither of vs can iuftly miflike their minifterie, that
is, the reading of the holy Scriptures, &c. Nowe I
come to your propofitions, which you call *Axiomes.*
The firft is this : viz. *Euery minifterie is expreffely fet
downe in the worde.* I graunt that the fubftance of euery minifterie is exprefly fet downe in the holy word.
By *Minifterie*, I vnderftand not onely the minifterie
of the word & Sacraments (as you doe in this place)
but that minifterie which concerneth the reliefe of
the poore, and the ciuill gouernement. For the Magiftrate is the minifter of God. *Rom. 13.* If *Magiftracie*
is Gods minifterie, and the fubftance of it expreffely fet downe in Gods booke, it is a good confequent
that *Magiftracie* is not a deuice of man, but an eccle-
                                                                                  fiafticall

fiafticall conftitution , prefcribed in the worde. Your fecond *Axiome* is this : viz. *Euerie ministerie of the newe Teftament is a preaching ministerie.* If you meane(as I thinke you doe) euery minifterie of the worde in the new Teftament, I diffent not from you. Nowe fir, to come a litle neerer you, I muft tell you that which either you knowe not, or diffemble, viz. that the lawes of this lande doe barre ignorant men from entring into the holy mĩnifterie : they are flat againft it. I offer you a branch of an Act of Parliamẽt to be confidered of. The wordes of the Act are thefe: viz. *That none fhall be made minifter or admitted to preach or minifter the Sacraments , being vnder the age of 24. yeeres, nor vnleffe he firft bring to the Bifhop of that Dio-ceffe from men knowen to the Bifhop to be of found religion, a teftimoniall both of his honeft life ,and of his profeſſing the doctrine expreffed in the faid Articles: nor, vnleffe he bee able to anfwere and render to the Ordinarie an accompt of his faith in Latine ,according to the faid Articles : or, haue fpeciall gift and habilitie to bee a preacher : nor fhall bee ad-mitted to the order of Deacon or minifterie, vnleffe he fhall firft fubfcribe to the faid Articles. Anno.13.Reg. Elizab. cap.12.* You fee by this, that the lawe of the lande re-quireth in him which is to be admitted to the holy minifterie, foundneffe in religion, gifts in fome mea-fure , and honeftie of life . They muft go together. Learning without godlineffe, is as a gold ring vpon a fwines fnoute. Godlineffe in a minifter , without learning, is, as a faire colour without light to fhew it by , and as a goodly bell without a clapper. Your third *Axoime* is this : viz. *The minifterie of our vnprea-ching minifters, is not a preaching minifterie .* No man doubteth of this , vnleffe he bee voyde of common

A a.iij.   fenfe.

senſe. Thus you haue my reſolution briefly for theſe poynts: and yet you are no conquerour, as *Cæſar* was, nor I ouerthrowen, as *Pompey* was. If your arguments were as tidie, as your ſpeeches are confident, there were no dealing with you. I perceiue the greateſt barkers are not the foreſt biters. Anſwere me I pray you directly to theſe queſtions. Doe you thinke, becauſe our vnpreaching miniſters are not preaching miniſters, that no ſacraments either were or are adminiſtred by them? Before, you denie it not. If you ſhould, neither ſacrifices nor ſacraments were offered or adminiſtred by your ignorāt Leuitical prieſts: for they were vnpreaching miniſters. Do you thinke that al ſuch are polluted, which receiue a Sacrament at the handes of vnpreaching miniſters? If you doe, then was Saint *Paul* polluted which communicated with your ignorant Leuites: for they were vnpreaching miniſters. Thus you ſee, to what ſtreights you are driuen.

CHAP. 25.

I. Penry.

THE MINISTERIE OF OVR
vnpreaching miniſters, is not a preaching miniſterie.

F the miniſterie of vnpreaching miniſters be a preaching miniſterie, or if their function be a paſtorall or doctoral function, then there had bene a preaching miniſtery, a paſtorall and doctorall function knowen in the Church, though there neuer had bene any preacher therein. Otherwiſe, howe can their miniſtery be a preaching miniſtery, or their function be a paſtorall function, whereas the ſame may be in the Church, no preaching miniſtery miniftery or paftorall function being knowen there? But no Church,much leffe a miniftery had there bene knowen, if there neuer had bene any that could haue preached: Becaufe God ordeined the Saints and fo a Church, onely to be gathered together by preaching ordinarily, but not by the miniftery of readers,becaufe it might haue bene in the worlde, & yet no faint gathered thereby: which thing experience in our Church prooueth to be too true.

R.Some.

You would thinke him ftrangely occupied, that fhould fet downe argumēts to proue that midnight is not high noone. Your labour is fuch in this particular: and you fweate & moyle in it very bufily. The gaine you are like to reape, is your labour for your trauaile.You write, that if no preaching had bene, no Church had bene. If you meane that no Church had ordinarily bene without preaching, that is, that preaching is the ordinarie means for the beginning and growth of the Church, I affent vnto you: but I adde this, that it hath and doeth pleafe God, by the reading of the holy Scriptures and the working of his Spirit, to renue the hearts of many. If you fhall anfwere that this courfe is not fo ordinarie as the other,I will accept your anfwere,and withall confeffe that in this point,no difference is betweene vs.

I.Penry.

My 2. and 3. reafons are drawen out of thefe wordes of Paul, Rom.12.6 7.8.Seeing then that we haue giftes that are diuers,according to the grace that is giuen vnto vs: whether we haue prophecie,let vs prophecie,according to the proportion of faith: or an office, let vs waite on the office: or he that teacheth on teaching, or he that exhorteth on exhorting,&c. The 2.reafon is thus concluded.

Whofoeuer hath receiued a miniftery, and fo a paftorall or doctorall function,hee hath receiued prophecie fpoken of in this place,verfe 6. Becaufe euery paftoral or doctorall function,mentioned in the 7.and 8.verfe, vnder thefe words, he that teacheth,hee that exhorteth: are conteined vnder the word prophecie,verf.6.Infomuch as he that hath not receiued that prophecie there fet downe,wherby is ment the interpretation of the word:

he

he hath not receiued the paftorall or doctoral function fet downe verf.7.8
But vnpreaching minifters haue not receiued the prophecie fpoken of in
this place,which is exprefly fet downe,verfe 6.to be one of the diuers gifts
beftowed for the gouernment of the body,which is the Church. Therefore
alfo,they haue receiued neither a paftoral nor a doctorall function,and fo
no preaching miniftery.

R.Some.

Your drifte is as before,to proue that our ignorant
minifters are vnfurnifhed, therefore no preachers.
You fay true.Will you conclude of this, that they
haue no minifterie at all,& that the actions of their
miniftery,viz. the adminiftration of the facraments,
the reading of the holy fcriptures,&c. are not profitable in any fort to the godly affebly? If you difpute
thus,I deny your argument,and do giue this reafon.
An abfurde Magiftrate is not furnifhed by almightie God,and therefore vtterly vnfit to be Gods lieu-
tenant: but we may not inferre of this,that the actes
done by him in his magiftracie are not the actes of
a Magiftrate. If you tell me that the arguments for
vnfit magiftrates & minifters are of feuerall ftamps,
I graunt you fay fo.So did,when time was, an other
groffe Anabaptift: but all learned men agree with
me,and diffent from you.

I.Penry.

3 No miniftery is feparated from a gift,becaufe prophecie fpoken of in
this 6.verfe,vnder which as we fee, euery paftorall and doctorall miniftery
is conteined,cannot bee feuered from a gift: but the miniftery of our readers is feuered in them from a gift: therefore in them it is no miniftery.

It is no miniftery in them I fay, although that miniftery, the generall
name whereof they haue,is not feuered from a gift in preaching minifters:
But what is that to them? what is the miniftery of other men vnto them?
they are not minifters, by the miniftery wherewith other men are endued,
but by their owne, which being feuered from a gift, is no miniftery. Paul
had bin no Apoftle,& had receiued no Apoftlefhip,vnleffe he could haue
fayd, I am a minifter according vnto the grace giuen vnto mee, *Ephe.3.7.*
and not according to the grace giuen vnto other Apoftles, the generall
name of whofe Apoftlefhip I am entituled with. A ridiculous fpeache it
were

were to fay,mine apoftlefhip hath receiued grace,but I that am the apoftle haue receiued none.

Howe then may our readers claime a preaching miniftery vnto themfelues, feeing the miniftery which they challenge,is altogether in them without a gift,though it be not fo in others?

R.Some.

I graunt that no lawfull and good Minifter of God wants furniture of gifts. If you will conclude of this, that the approbation of the Church is nothing if fufficiét parts be wanting in them which are admitted to the minifterie, I denie your argument, and doe offer you for my reafon a floure of your owne garden: euen that which you haue written before in thefe wordes,viz.that *vnfitneffe to teach made not a nullitie of the Leuitical priefts office.*If you anfwere that extreeme ignorance in the Leuiticall prieftes, did neither barre them from, nor ftrippe them of the Leuiticall priefthood: I replie that this is a pofitiue and perpetual law of almightie God for the prieftes then,& for the Minifters now,viz. *The priefts lips fhall keepe knowledge.Mal.2.*yea,M.*Caluine* a famous learned man writeth vpon that place of *Malachie,*that *Sacerdos & doctor funt termini conuertibiles*, that is,that Gods prieft & a teacher are fo neere of kinne, that they are like to *Hippocrates* twinnes, which laughed together and wept together, which liued together and died together. You adde that the minifterie in preaching minifters is not feuered from a gift: but that the vnpreaching minifter is not enriched by the furniture of another mans gifts.A deepe matter forfooth. It is as cleare as the Sunne,that learned minifters haue furniture of gifts, & that ignorant men are not learned becaufe the other are fo. Blind *Bartimeus* could haue efpied this.Do you thinke that

Bb. any

any man of any accompt for learning will reafon thus? Diuers learned men haue written excellently, therefore M.*Penry* hath fo, which hath broched many palpable errours. If any fhould difpute
thus, he fhould reafon abfurdly : and yet it is as wife
a fpeech as that which was deliuered euen nowe by
your felfe. You write that it were a ridiculous fpeach
to fay, Mine Apoftlefhip hath receiued grace, but I
that am the Apoftle, haue receiued none. I confeffe
that Gods graces are not tied to any chaire. To
thinke otherwife, is a popifh fancie. But I dare tell
you this, which I am fure is good diuinitie, that fome
actions of ignorant & euill minifters may haue good
grace at Gods hands, when the parties themfelues
find none. I prooue it thus. Firft, the facrifices of ignorant Leuiticall prieftes were profitable to many
godly men in that time, but not to thofe priefts. Secondly, publique prayers deliuered by abfurd minifters in the name of the godly affembly, are profitable to the affembly, but not to them : for the
prayers are accepted by almightie God, *Non pro per-
uerfitate præpofitorum, fed pro deuotione populorum*, that
is, Not for the peruerfeneffe of the minifters, but for
the deuotion of the people. *Augu. contra epift. Parm.
libr.2.cap.8.*

I.Penry.

Euery vnpreaching minifter finneth in executing the workes of a paftorall function, as the Sacraments, &c. therefore he hath no miniftery, and fo
neither a paftorall nor doctorall function. He hath no miniftery, becaufe
his calling is not the calling of the miniftery. His calling is not the calling
of the miniftery, becaufe he finneth in intermedling with the works thereof. And this is an infallible trueth, that no man finneth becaufe he dealeth
with the workes of his calling. For this is the ductie that God requireth at
the hands of euery man. Many finne in deede becaufe they walke corruptly in their callings, and haue no care to glorifie God therein, Col.3.17. But
leaue thy corruption and thou finneft not, in keeping thee to the workes of
                                                                              thy

thy calling. The hypocrites in the dayes of Iſaiah 1.13. ſinned not becauſe they offered ſacrifice, but becauſe they did the ſame through hypocriſie. Their hypocriſie they ought to haue left, but not his ſeruice in ſacrificing according to his commandement: but our readers though they ſhould with as litle corruption, and as great zeale to Gods glory and the good of his Church as any men, deale in the workes of a paſtorall miniſtery, yet they ſhould ſtill doe that which the Lord had forbidden them to doe, whence it appeareth, that the workes of the miniſtery are not the workes of their calling. For God forbiddeth no man to deale therewith, and not being the workes of their calling, they are no miniſters, and haue neyther paſtorall nor doctorall function.

R. Some.

You would fayne prooue that vnpreaching miniſters haue no miniſterie at all: but it will not be. You haue euill lucke: you cannot hitte that marke. Your reaſon is this: *Euerie vnpreaching miniſter ſinneth in executing the workes of a paſtorall function, as the Sacraments &c. therefore he hath no miniſterie &c.* Mine anſwere is, that I deny your argument. My reaſon is: The ſonnes of *Heli* ſinned in the execution of their miniſtery, *1.Sam.2.* yet they were miniſters. The contentious miniſters of *Philippi* ſinned in the execution of their miniſterie, *Philippi.1.* yet they were miniſters. You go on M. *Penry* in this ſort: The Lord, you ſay, hath forbidden ignorant men to deale with the workes of the miniſterie, therefore ignorant miniſters haue no miniſterie at all. Your Antecedent is true: for the holy miniſterie is too high a calling for ſuch baſe companions. Your argument is very falſe. My reaſon is: your ignorant Leuites were forbidden by almightie God to enter into the prieſthood: yet they were lawfull prieſts in your iudgement, becauſe they were of the line of *Aaron* &c.

I. Penry.

This is further ſhewed, foraſmuch as the Lord doeth not commit vnto bare readers the charge of thoſe ſoules, ouer whom they are, which he doeth vnto euery one that hath a paſtorall function, Acts.20.26.28. 1.theſ.

5.12.Heb.13.17. For to what ende elſe, ſhould he commit a miniſterie vnto any, who haue ſoules vnder their charge? The Church in deede may commit the ſoules of men vnto readers, but certainely the Lord committeth none vnto them. And he is no miniſter, vnto whom the Lord doeth not commit this charge, as the places before quoted doe ſhewe. For the Lord hath in his word, ordeined not onely offices, the executours whereof ſhould haue the ouerſight of ſoules, but alſo the perſons who were to execute thoſe funĉtions,1.Cor.12.28. 1.Pet.4.10.Rom,12,6.7.8. Epheſ.4.7. 11. Nowe vnpreaching miniſters are none of thoſe perſons, becauſe the Lord knoweth them not to be able to feede ſoules. And let not men be ſo iniurious vnto the Lord, as to affirme, that he according vnto his reuealed ordinance (for thereof I ſpeake as of a miniſterie, and not of his ſecret iudgements) bequeathed the ſoules of men to be ſtarued and kept from ſaluation. As he muſt needs be conuinced, to do if he bequeathed thē vnto thoſe men, the diſpenſatiō of whoſe miniſterie is able to beget none, feede none, ſaue none. You muſt vnderſtand againe, that I ſpeake of the miniſterie whereby readers are miniſters, that is, of their owne, and not of the miniſterie whereby preaching miniſters are miniſters, wherewith readers haue nothing to doe.

R.*Some*.

That almightie God neuer committed charge of ſoules to ignorant men (vnleſſe it were to puniſh them, as he did the rebellious Iſraelites by ignorant Leuiticall prieſtes) is a cleare trueth in diuinitie: I agree with you in that. You ſay that the diſpenſation of our readers miniſterie doth feede none. In that you erre groſſely. My reaſon is: The Sacraments adminiſtred by them doe comfort and feede the ſoules of the godly communicants: for the vertue of the Sacrament dependeth not of any miniſter whatſoeuer &c. The ſcriptures read by vnpreaching miniſters do edifie the aſſemblie which is reuerētly attētiue. If you anſwer that the word ſoundly preached doth edifie more, I aſſent. If you deny that the ſcriptures read by vnpreaching miniſters do edifie in any ſort, you ſpeake blaſphemouſly, & I haue refuted that abſurditie, *Chap.4.* of this treatiſe. There is great difference betweene the Miniſter and miniſterie: but either you cannot or will not ſee it.

*I.*Penry.

I. Penry.

Moreouer, howe can the Lord be fayd to commit the charge of foules, according to his owne reuealed ordinance, vnto thofe who may truely obiect vnto him, that he dealeth iniurioufly with them, by exacting thofe things to be perfourmed at their hands and in their owne perfons, as neceffary duties of their callings, vnto the performance whereof, they haue receiued no abilitie from him? Is man to be anfwerable vnto the Lord of that which he neuer receiued? doeth the Lord require the vfe of that talent which he neuer beftowed? doth he lay that vpon any, whereof he may haue iuft caufe to complaine? When did he impofe a charge vpon any, vnto whom he gaue not gifts to difcharge the fame? nowe the charge of foules which he committeth vnto any, he requireth at their hands vnto whom he hath committed it, which he could not doe, if he had not giuen abilitie to the difcharge thereof.

R. Some.

I haue proued before, *Chap.2.* that almightie God furnifhed fuch as he called to the holy minifterie in the old and newe Teftament. I reft in that. If his Maieftie (which is farre from him) either had or did commit the charge of foules to fuch as haue no mettall in them, hee might be iuftly conuinced of, and chaléged for iniurious dealing with them. No good Captaine will fend his fouldier naked into the fielde againft an armed enemie. You write that God dealeth iniurioufly with men, by exacting thofe things to bee performed at their handes and in their owne perfons as neceffary dueties of their callings, vnto the performance whereof, they haue receiued no abilitie from him, &c. You referre this fpeach, I am fure, to the Minifters. To take you otherwife, were to wring your words, and to mifconftrue you. I wil not offer you fuch meafure: therefore I leaue you a litle while, and do tel the godly Reader that the *Pelagians* in *Auguftines* time, and the Papifts in our time, reafon in this fort: Almightie God requireth nothing at our hands, vnto the performance whereof he hath not giuen abilitie: therefore the regenerate are able

B b. iij.   to

to fulfill the Law of God in this life. This argument was and is accompted of the *Pelagians* and *Papiſts* an inuincible reaſon: but it is a very ſimple one. I denie the Antecedent,&c. The reaſon is : God requireth of vs the fulfilling of the Lawe : but, the regenerate are not able to fulfill it. That this point may bee better vnderſtanded, I will ſet downe my propoſiti-on and reaſons, in the ende of this booke.

I.Penry.

What then ? ſhall ignorant miniſters be free from the blood of ſoules, in aſmuch as the Lorde neuer committed any ſoule vnto their charge? It were well with them poore men, if the caſe ſo ſtood. But alas it is not ſo. And yet the cauſe of their deſtruction proceedeth not from their vnfaith-fulnes in the diſcharge of that vocation which he hath allotted vnto thē, but it commeth iuſtly vpon them, in that they haue deſperatly thruſt them ſelues contrary vnto Gods reuealed will, vpon thoſe men, with the ouer-ſight of whoſe ſoules God neuer truſted ſuch as they are. The Lorde ſayth vnto them, intrude your ſelues and you will, vnto the places of paſtors, and ſo enforce me to bring heauy and ſwift damnation vpon you: but ſure-ly I will bequeath no ſoule vnto your cuſtodie. They on the other ſide in their practiſe ſay, Lord whether thou committeſt vnto vs any charge of a-ny ſoule or no, we care not, but rather then we ſhould not haue ỹ meanes to liue in this life, (for this is their onely ſcope in continuing in the mini-ſterie) require the blood of ſoules, and what thou wilt at our hands. And ſo ſenſeles men, they ſell themſelues, body and ſoule vnto euerlaſting wo and deſtruction.

R.Some.

I am ſo farre from being a defence to ignorant, ei-ther Leuits before, or Miniſters now, that I confeſſe freely that their entrance into the prieſthoode and miniſterie, and continuance in it moſt abſurdly, was and is a greeuous ſinne. If the Lord hath or ſhall pu-niſh them ſeuerely for their intruſion into ſo high a calling, they cannot plead *not guiltie.* If they doe, it is in vaine : for, at Gods barre they ſhall not be acqui-ted. You write that the ignorant miniſters, whome you call ſenſeleſſe men, doe ſell themſelues bodie

and

and foule to euerlafting deftruction. Your fpeech is true : *Illi viderint:* Let them, if they be not graceleffe and fhameleffe, looke vnto it. All that I fay vnto it, is : the Lord for his Chrifts fake heale that fore. It is not fo grieuous, thankes be to God, as it was : I affure my felfe, it will bee leffe : I woulde to God it were none.

I.Penry.

The pretence that the Lord committeth the charge of foules vnto their minifterie, and not vnto them, is firft a defiring of that in queftion : (for they are denied to haue any minifterie) and otherwife many wayes vnfufficient. 1 Becaufe the Lord committeth not the charge of foules there, where the punifhment of their deftruction cannot take holde, as it can not vpon the minifterie : 2 the minifterie is but a dead thing of it felfe, moft beautifull in deede, as being an ordinance of the Lorde, but able to faue none, vnleffe it be committed vnto a perfon, who in the execution thereof, is able to fhewe himfelfe to be appointed of God for that glorious worke. This is taught Ephef.4. where the Apoftle verfes 6. and 7. hauing fpoken of the giftes beftowed vpon men for this minifteriall worke, afcribeth verf. 11.12. the gathering together of the Saints, not vnto the giftes or functions, but vnto men endued with the faid gifts. For he doth not fay that the Lord hath appointed for the gathering together of the Saints, an apoftlefhip, a paftorall or doctorall function, &c. but that he ordained apoftles, paftors, &c. for that end and puipofe : whereunto becaufe our readers were not appointed, it forcibly enfueth, that they haue no minifterie, no paftorall or doctorall function, and fo are no minifters : which conclufion alfo in the laft edition of mine exhortation vnto my countreymen, I haue enforced by many ftrong, and as I am affured inuincible reafons, drawen out of the infallible trueth of Gods worde.

R.Some.

What other men doe or will pretende, I cannot tell. I am fully perfwaded, that Almightie God did neuer commit his fheepe, fouldiers, citie, to foolifh fhepheards, vnskilfull captaines, blinde watchmen. Such fhepheards, captaines, watchmen, were your ignorant Leuiticall Priefts, whofe entrance and continuance in the priefthoode, are condemned by the written worde. The line of *Aaron* was not ftrong ynough to breake the cords of Almightie God. Such fhepheards,captaines, watchmen, are our ignorant minifters. Let the ignorant Leuites and minifters be matched together, good *M.Penry.* They muft needes faile in one fhippe, fight vnder one banner, and bee condemned at one barre: and yet I graunt, that your ignorant Leuites which were neuer called of God, but of the Iewifh Church, did offer and deliuer the Legal Sacrifices and Sacraments: and that the godly Communicants were not polluted by their ignorance. You muft of force graunt me thus much for vnpreaching minifters: for you haue not before denied it. So fhall fome queftions betweene you and me be decided, and you fhall agree with all the learned Proteftants and reformed Churches. You write that the Apoftle doth not fay that the Lord hath appointed for the gathering together of the Saintes, an Apoftlefhip, a paftorall or doctorall function, but that he ordeined apoftles, paftors, &c. You write ftrangely in my iudgement. If God appointed Apoftles, he appointed the Apoftlefhip: if paftors, he appointed a paftorall function : for they cannot be fingled. Euery meane Logician, yea euery fenfible man conceiueth this.

I. Penry.

I woulde intreate you, *M Some,* when you haue anfwered the reafons I haue nowe fet downe, to anfwere alfo the 1.2.3. and 25. reafon that I haue there vfed. For you fhall but ftriue in vaine againft the conclufion, as long as the premiffes, whereby it is inferred, remaine firme. If the Reader would be further fatisfied in this point concerning the dumbe Minifterie, he is to be referred vnto that which in the aforefaid Treatife I haue fet downe.

R.Some.

I haue now anfwered your whole booke. I haue and doe fubmit my labour to the iudgement of the learned, therefore not of you or your ignorant difciples. Becaufe you will haue mee haue a little more
worke,

worke,you intreate mee to anſwere foure reaſons in
your *Addition.* If you had not bene very lordly, you
would haue ſet downe the reaſons your ſelfe : but,
whatſoeuer you doe , becommeth you . You may
commaund, comptroll , and deale with others, as
Strato did, which was a king ouer beaſts. At the leaſt,
you thinke ſo, whatſoeuer other men doe . Well, I
am content to ſatisfie your deſire: for, as good happe
is, I haue your booke by me : and it is a fault *in extre-*
*mo actu deficere,*that is, to reſemble the ſlouthful poet
in the winding vp of the clewe. Your firſt reaſon is
conteined in theſe wordes : viz. Euery one that hath
the life of a miniſter good or bad (or that is a miniſter in deede) is ordayned of God for the gathering
together of the Saints : For, there is no other miniſter ſpoken of in the worde. No bare reader is ordeined of God for this ende : Therefore no bare reader
is a miniſter in deede, or hath the life of a miniſter,
good or bad. In *Add.pag.52.* I anſwere briefly, that
ſome parts of your Maior propoſition are without
ſenſe. You write that euery one which hath the life
of a bad miniſter is ordained of God for the gathering together of the Saints, In this ſhort ſpeech of
yours, there are groſſe errors. The firſt errour is, that
bad miniſters are ordeined of God for the gathering
together of the Saints. It is a certaine truth in Gods
booke, that ſuch as are called by the Lord to this excellent worke , are not bad miniſters, as you verie
baſely do imagine, but choiſe men for gifts and life,
&c. *1.Tim.3.* Your ſecond errour, is this : viz . That
furniture of gifts is one part of the life of a bad miniſter. This is ſtrange diuinitie. My reaſon is : furniture
of gifts is one part of the life of a good miniſter : ther-

fore

fore want of giftes is one branch of the life of a bad
minifter. The Antecedent is manifeſt : the argument is ſtrong: *ſecundùm legem oppoſitionis*, as the Logicians tearme it. I haue told you often, that furniture of giftes is of the eſſence of a lawfull and good
minifter of God, but not of the eſſence of a minifter
ſimply. This I reſt in : ſo muſt you whether you will
or no, vnleſſe you will crie downe your ignorant Leuites, and holde this for a principle, that no Sacrament, either was or is adminiſtred by vnpreaching
minifters. Your three other reaſons, are all one, and
may be ſhut vp in this ſhort argument : viz. *Vnprea-*
ching miniſters are not able to feede the elect with the food
of knowledge and vnderſtanding : therefore they haue no
calling at all, howſoeuer they haue the Churches approbati-
on, &c. In Add.pag.55.57. I denie your argument, and
haue ſet downe reaſons for it before, in this Treatiſe. It is time now to take *manum de tabula,* that
is, to ceaſe this courſe. My comfort is, that
I haue the conſent of all the learned,
and that Almightie God wil
bleſſe this labour.

The

The regenerate are not able to fulfill the Lawe of God.

¶ *My reasons are.*

He Law is a yoke, which neither the holy Fathers, nor the Apostles,&c. were able to beare. So saith the Apostle *Peter* in that famous Councill holden at *Ierusalem*: his words are these, *Why tempt ye God, to lay a yoke on the disciples neckes, which neither our Fathers, nor wee were able to beare, &c. Acts.chap.*15.*verse* 10.11. *S Peter* speaketh expresly of such as were regenerate.

2 It was impossible to the Lawe (to take away sinne and death) in as much as it was weake because of the flesh. So writeth S.*Paul Rom.*8. therefore the weakenesse of flesh is such euen in the regenerate, that they are not able to fulfill the Lawe. *Lex iubet, non iuuat: offendit peccatum, non tollit:* that is, the Lawe doth commaund, but not helpe: the Lawe doth shewe sinne, but it doth not take away sinne.

3 The regenerate are guiltie of the breach of some one commaundement: therefore they doe not fulfill the Lawe.

The antecedent is manifest, for the regenerate doe sinne, 1.Iohn 1.8. Matth.6.12. *Non peccare, Dei iustitia:* that is, not to sinne is Gods righteousnesse &c. and sinne is a transgression of the Lawe, 1.Iohn 3 I proue my argument thus: *He that faileth in one (commaundement) is guiltie of all. Iames* 2.10. The reason of that is, First, because he hath violated the maiestie of the Lawgiuer which is one and the same: Secondly, because the body of Gods Lawe is *indiuiduum,* that is, cannot be parted.

4 The workes of the regenerate, are vnperfite. *Aaron* which was the high Priest, in the time of the Lawe, and a figure of Christ, was appointed by Almightie God, to beare the iniquitie of the holy offrings, *Exod. Chap.* 28.*verse* 38. S. *Paul* after his conuersion, was farre from perfection, *Phil. Chap.*3. The same Apostle writeth thus of himselfe: *I knowe nothing by my selfe, yet am I not thereby iustified.* 1.*Cor. Chap.*4. *verse* 4. *Ad eius examen vita nostra ducitur, sub quo & virtutes nostrae trepidant:* that is, our life is examined by him (that is, Almightie God) before whom our vertues tremble: So writeth *Anselmus,* which was sometimes Archbishop of *Canterburie,* in his Commentarie vpon 1.*Corinth. Chap.*4.

5 The regenerate cannot loue God & their neighbour perfectly, as the Lawe of God requireth: for they offend God and their neighbour, either in worde, deede, or concupiscence, therefore, &c. *The Law is spirituall, Rom. Chap.*7. that is, bindeth our hearts as well as our bodies to obedience. *Who can say, (truely) my heart is cleane? Pro. Chap.*20. *Who can tell how oft he offendeth? Psal.*19. *In quibusdam iustos suos quoniam ad huc extolli possunt, non adiuuat ad perficiendam iustitiam, vt dum non iustificatur in conspectu eius omnis viuens, actionem gratiarum semper indulgentiae ipsius debeamus: & sic ab illa prima causa omniu vitioru, id est à tumore superbiae, sancta humilitate sanemur. August de peccat. mer. & remiss. contra Pelag. lib.*3.*cap.*13. The summe of Augustines

guftines wordes is, that becaufe iuft men may growe prowde, Almightie God doth not affift them in fome particulers to perfite righteoufnes, that they may be thankfull for his mercie, and decline pride, &c.

6 *The Scripture doth conclude all vnder finne, that the promife, that is, euer-lafting inheritance, by the faith of Iefus Chrift, fhoulde be giuen to them that be-leeue, Galath.Chap.3.verfe 22.*

Queftion.

If we cannot fulfill the lawe of God, what vfe haue we of the lawe?

Anfvere.

By the lawe we vnderftand Gods pleafure more certainely. *Pfal.*19. by the lawe, wee vnderftand our nakednesse, as we doe our debts by an obli-gation, and our fpots by the looking glaffe. *The lawe is a fchoolemafter to bring vs to Chrift. Galath.chap.3.verfe* 24. which Chrift is a furgeon and phi-fician to the wounded and difeafed.

Queftion.

Howe are we iuft in Gods fight?

Anfvere.

By Chrifts righteoufneffe: which is ours by imputation, as our finnes were Chrifts by imputation. The Apoftle writeth that *Chrift is our righ-teoufneffe.1.Corinth.chap.1.*

It is confeffed both by proteftants and papifts, that wee are iuftified by *Grace*. The difference betweene vs is in this. The proteftants by this word (*Grace*) vnderftand Gods fauour, whereby our finnes are pardoned : by which meere and onely *Grace* and mercy of God in Chrift, we are iuftifi-ed in Gods fight. The papifts by this word (*Grace*) vnderftand a quality powred into our hearts by Almightie God : by reafon of which qualitie we liue holily and are iuftified (as they fay) in Gods fight. This is the *Inherent righteoufneffe* which the papifts doe write and fpeake fo much of. Wee which are the proteftants, do confeffe, that that righteoufneffe, which is an effect of Gods fanctifying fpirit, and the fruite of our iuftification before God, is inherent in vs : likewife the firft fruits of our glorification, that is, peace of confcience & ioy in the holy Ghoft. That righteoufneffe wherby we are accompted iuft, or are iuftified, or are made iuft before God, is not inherent in vs, my reafon is : we are made righteous by Chrifts obedience. *Rom.chap.5.verf.19.* which obedience of Chrift, is not within, but without vs : and yet this obedience of Chrift, is apprehended by a iuftifying faith, as almes is by the hand of a poore man. Perfite righteoufnes fhould be in-herent in vs, if we could keepe all Gods commaundements as exactly, as Almightie God requireth. The beft men were and are fhort in that. One-ly our Lord and fauiour Iefus Chrift, which was free from finne, did fulfill the lawe as God requireth.

Iuftitia noftra potiùs conftat remiffione peccatorum, quàm perfectione virtutum: that is, our righteoufneffe doth confift rather in for-giueneffe of finnes, then in perfection of vertues. *Auguft.de ci-uit : dei.lib.19.cap.27.*

FINIS.